FINDING THE KINGDOM

Brian Leonard

FINDING GOD'S KINGDOM ON EARTH TODAY

This book contains
The Word of God
Which is powerful enough
To change your heart
And your life

He who has ears
Let him hear.

To read the Bible in English go to:
https://www.biblestudytools.com/

Chapter 1 – Are you happy?

Everyone wants to be happy. Yet happiness is a state of mind that may only last a few moments. On a scale, with sadness on one side, and happiness on the other, most of us spend the day fluctuating around the middle. In this state, you are comfortable with your environment and your activity. Your environment is the people and places that surround you and with which you interact. Your activity is what you do in that environment.

There is a third equally as important factor that effects your ability to be happy and that is your disposition. This is defined as your mood, nature or temperament. Some will say that your disposition is mainly influenced by your DNA which you were given at birth and which cannot be changed. This book teaches you how to have a positive disposition towards yourself and the world through faith in Jesus Christ. Your disposition or temperament can be changed through faith.

Each of us, is starting our journey through this book from a different starting point determined by our past. Your background may be Muslim, Hindu, Buddhist, Atheist or Hebrew. You might start with a hatred of Christianity or a complete indifference. The fact that you have read this far shows that you are searching for more in life. I believe that God put that 'wanting something different' into your heart.

Chapter 2 – Where to Start

You believe in something. An atheist believes there is no God. All the quotes in this book come from the Bible. If you do not believe in the Bible, please be patient and listen to what it says. This is what the Bible says about itself:

Blessed (Favoured by God) is the one who keeps the words of the prophecy written in this scroll (the Bible). Revelations 22.7

So, if there is a God of the Bible, he wants you to understand what is written in it.

The next question is whether you believe in God. The Bible says:

Since what may be known about God is plain to them (people), because God has made it plain to them. For since the creation of the world, God's invisible qualities – his eternal power and divine nature – have been clearly seen, being understood from what he has made so that people are without excuse. Romans 1.19-20

God says, just look at the world around you, that, in itself, is evidence that I exist. The sheer beauty, symmetry and diversity of the natural world around you are proof that there is a God.

There are two possibilities: either there is a God, or there is not. If there is no God, then there is no judgement at the end of your life. If there is no judgement, it does not matter what you do in this life, as long as you do not get caught. You could murder, steal, rape and provided you were not found out, you would get away with it.

Society could make up what laws it liked. It would decide what is right or wrong. Since there was no God, we could make laws to persecute the Jews, segregate the black and victimise the poor. Countries who implement these policies, might be condemned by other countries, but since there is no God, they would not be judged for them in any after life.

Psychologists would argue that we have a built-in sense of right and wrong (moral truth). When we talk about moral truth, we mean that we know instinctively that something is right or wrong. If there is no God, there is no good and evil only man's instinct of what is good and evil.

But if there is a God, He must have some form of power, otherwise he would not be a God. Since man can communicate with man, God must also be able to communicate with man. What God has communicated with man throughout history? The God in the Bible has.

This is what the Bible says about God:

He heals the broken-hearted and binds up their wounds. He determines the number of the stars and calls them each by name. Great is our Lord and mighty in power; his understanding has no limit. Psalm 147.3-5

He made the earth by his power; he founded the world by his wisdom and stretched out the heavens by his understanding. Jeremiah 51.15

You are worthy, our Lord and God, to receive glory and honour and power, for you created all things, and by your will they were created and have their being. Revelations 4.11

You are a gracious and compassionate God, slow to anger and abounding in love. Jonah 4.2

Wow. If the God of the Bible exists, he has all the qualities you would expect a God to have glory, honour, power, wisdom, understanding and love. The Bible says that God is Love:

God is love. Whoever lives in love lives in God, and God in them. 1 John 4.16

This God is so full of love that he made the world to share it with us. But God did not stop there. When we disobeyed him and went away from him, he sent his own Son to save us:

For God so loved the world that he gave his one and only Son, that whoever believes in him shall not perish but have eternal life. John 3.16

Annex 1 sets out a case against evolution and for there being a Creator.

To read each chapter of the New Testament, go to this site and enter the chapter title in the search facility: https://www.biblestudytools.com/

Chapter 3 – Was Jesus the Son of God?

There is sufficient historic evidence from several different sources to confirm that Jesus existed and was crucified. Not many people dispute that Jesus existed.

There is written evidence from different sources other than the Bible to confirm this.

The central message of the New Testament is to Believe in Jesus. If the Bible is the Word of God, God would give you as much evidence as He thinks you need to believe. No matter how much evidence God is going to give non-believers, they still will not believe. Believers and potential believers will always listen to the evidence because they are always looking to justify their faith.

Historic Evidence

History is based on evidence, mostly of eyewitnesses who record the events. The more witnesses (sources) and the better their character, the more reliable the evidence. The evidence that Jesus was not raised from the dead is the one report of the soldiers that his disciples stole the body while they were asleep (Matthew 28.13). If they were asleep how did they know the body was stolen? The clothes that Jesus' body was wrapped in, were folded neatly in the tomb. It is very unlikely that grave robbers would have been so neat while stealing a body with soldiers outside.

 Against this, we have six witnesses that recorded the eleven times that he was seen alive at separate events over a forty-day period after his death.

He appeared to Cephas, and then to the Twelve. After that, he appeared to more than five hundred of the brothers and sisters at the same time, most of whom are still living, though some have fallen

asleep. Then he appeared to James, then to all the apostles, and last of all he appeared to me also (Paul). (1 Corinthians 15. 5 – 8).

Sightings were also recorded in Mark (16.9), Matthew (28.9), Luke (24.15) and John (21.1).
If this was fake news, the five of them would have had to conspire together to record it. Remembering the commands that Jesus taught, it is unlikely that these men would deliberately break a commandment and lie. They would have no motive to lie. Jesus being alive would make their lives much more difficult, otherwise, they could have gone back to their old lives.

Jesus' first appearance to Mary Magdalene demonstrates Jesus' compassion (John 20.11 and Mark 16.9). She was sitting in the garden outside the tomb completely distraught, because the body was missing.

Jesus said to her, "Mary." She turned toward him and cried out in Aramaic, "Rabboni!" (which means "Teacher"). John 20.16

Evidence from Modern Day Miracles

The proof that Jesus is the Son of God is evident from the miracles that are done in his name in today's modern world. Jesus said if you don't believe in me believe from the evidence of my works (John 14.11). Doubters would question the miracles, but there is no logical explanation for many of them other than faith in Jesus. Many of them cannot be proved, but others where a doctor or consultant has made a diagnosis and the illness has completely disappeared following the diagnosis are unexplainable.

Jesus has done three miracles in my life which I do not dispute. Doctors diagnosed, by taking several biopsies over a period, that I had irreversible destructive cell changes in my oesophagus (Barrett's oesophagus). When the time came for hospital treatment, the doctors found that my oesophagus had healed. An occurrence that they could not explain. I know in my heart Jesus healed me. This is only one small example there are many more on the internet and on YouTube.

The following website has video clips of many modern-day miracles done in Jesus' name: www.godisreal.today/modern-day-miracles. A must see video on you tube: Our daughter's heart stopped then Jesus walked in.

The YouTube video - The Last Reformation The Beginning (2016) - shows many modern day miracles done in the name of Jesus through the power of the Holy Spirit.

Evidence from Modern-day Testimonies

If you go on YouTube, you will see many testimonies of people who have come to Jesus. There are Hebrews, Muslims, Hindus, Buddhists and Christians (not born again) who are turning to Jesus for help. Each testimony is evidence of God's power to change lives. Each day, evil grows in the world, but good grows also. Like the yeast in the bread (Luke 13.21), the Kingdom of God is growing.

What God says about Jesus

 Twice in the New Testament, God speaks directly to us. He tells us that Jesus is his Son whom he loves. He also tells us to listen to him.

And a voice from the cloud said, "This is my Son, whom I love; with him I am well pleased. Listen to him!"
Mathew 17.5

As soon as Jesus was baptised, he went up out of the water. At that moment heaven was opened, and he saw the Spirit of God descending like a dove and alighting on him. And a voice from heaven said, "This is my Son, whom I love; with him I am well pleased."   Matthew 3.16-17

God tells you to listen to Jesus.

Chapter 4 – What Jesus did for You.

Jesus died on the cross for you because he loves you. The Bible says:

The Lord Jesus Christ gave himself for our sins to rescue us from the present evil age, according to the will of our God and Father. Galatians 1.3-4

He himself bore our sins in his body on the cross, so that we might die to sins and live for righteousness; by his wounds you have been healed. 1 Peter 2.23

The sins of
the world

God's punishment
for our sins

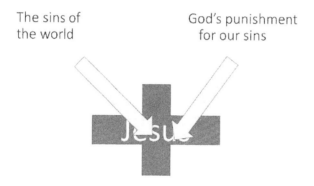

Surely, he took up our pain and bore our suffering, yet we considered him punished by God, stricken by him, and afflicted.   But he was pierced for our transgressions, he was crushed for our iniquities; the punishment that brought us peace was on him, and by his wounds we are healed. Isaiah 53.4 - 5

You (Jesus) were slain, and with your blood you purchased for God persons from every tribe and language and people and nation. Revelations 5.9

Jesus died for your sins. His blood was the price that he paid to rescue you. In order to be saved from this world, you need to believe that Jesus died on the cross and rose again.

This is love: not that we loved God, but that he loved us and sent his Son as an atoning sacrifice for our sins. 1 John 4.10

Just as the Son of Man did not come to be served, but to serve, and to give his life as a ransom for many. Matthew 20.28

This is good, and pleases God our Saviour, who wants all people to be saved and to come to a knowledge of the truth. For there is one God and one mediator between God and mankind, the man Christ Jesus, who gave himself as a ransom for all people. 1 Timothy 2. 3-6

For you know that it was not with perishable things such as silver or gold that you were redeemed from the empty way of life handed down to you from your ancestors, but with the precious blood of Christ, a lamb without blemish or defect. 1 Peter 1.18

Christ loved us and gave himself up for us as a fragrant offering and sacrifice to God. Ephesians 5.2

And having died for you, God raised him on the third day:

God raised him from the dead and glorified him. 1 Peter 1.21

But Christ has indeed been raised from the dead, the first fruits of those who have fallen asleep. For since death came through a man, the resurrection of the dead comes also through a man. For as in Adam all die, so in Christ all will be made alive. 1 Corinthians 15.20-22

Jesus rising from the dead is the greatest event in history. If it did not happen, we are all dead without any hope. If it happened, there is hope of life for everyone because Jesus died and rose again for everyone. Believe in Jesus and you are part of that hope.

And he ascended into heaven:

He (Jesus) was taken up before their very eyes, and a cloud hid him from their sight. This same Jesus, who has been taken from you into heaven, will come back in the same way you have seen him go into heaven. Acts 1. 9-11

Chapter 5 - Ask and Receive Jesus into your Heart.

<u>Jesus Christ, My Lord and my Saviour,</u>

<u>Thank you for dying for me on the cross and rising again,</u>

<u>I am sorry for my sins,</u>

<u>Jesus please come into my heart and save me.</u>

<u>Amen</u>

If you said that prayer and really meant it, you have become a follower of Jesus. Believing in Jesus will change your disposition and your attitude to yourself and the people around you. Jesus will put love into your heart.

And everyone who calls on the name of the Lord will be saved. Acts 2.21

<u>If you confess with your mouth, "Jesus is Lord" and believe in your heart that God raised Him from the dead, you will be saved.</u> <u>Romans 10.9</u>

Ask and it will be given you.
Seek and you will find.

Knock and the door will be opened to you.
Matthew 7.7

Ask God to give you the faith to believe in Jesus Christ.
Knock on Jesus' door and ask him to come into your life.
Ask God, the Father, Yahweh, to give you the Holy
Spirit and he will send the Holy Spirit into your heart.

**Yet to all who did receive him, to those who believed
in his name, he gave the right to become children of
God.** John 1.12

You now have the right to become a child of God. Wow.

It was God, the Father's decision to send Jesus Christ
into the world to save you.

**For you (God, the Father) granted him (Jesus Christ)
authority over all people that he might give eternal
life to all those you have given him.** John 17.2

God, the Father, gave you to Jesus and Jesus gave you
everlasting life because Jesus Christ has authority over
all people.

If you believe that Jesus Christ is the Son of God, you
will have eternal life. You will become a child of God.

Chapter 6 – Believe in Jesus.

For God so loved the world that he gave his one and only Son, that whoever believes in him shall not perish but have eternal life. John 3.16

This is God's wonderful promise to you. If you believe in Jesus, you will be saved. It tells us that God loves the whole world including those people that reject his love. The offer is to everybody. If you accept the offer, you enter God's love. You are justified before God. If you reject the offer, you stand condemned. Not to believe in Jesus is a sin which will lead to your soul being condemned to hell on judgement day.

If you believe you will be saved. But with belief comes a box full of treasures that God has given those that believe in his one and only Son.

Righteousness

This righteousness is given through faith in Jesus Christ to all who believe. Romans 3.22

Their faith is credited as righteousness. Romans 4. 5

You have become right with God. You are now justified and made right before God. You have received righteousness through your faith in Jesus. In Matthew 5, it tells you to seek God's righteousness each day by following Jesus. Your spirit is alive because of righteousness. You need to stay right with God each day of your life.

Peace

Therefore, since we have been justified through faith, we have peace with God through our Lord Jesus Christ. Romans 5.1

Jesus said, Peace I leave with you; my peace I give you. I do not give to you as the world gives. Do not let your hearts be troubled and do not be afraid. John 14.27

Jesus Christ took the punishment that bought us peace with God on the cross.

Grace

We have gained access through faith into this grace in which we stand. Romans 5.2

You now stand in Jesus' grace. Grace is the favour, love, mercy and protection given to you by God through Jesus because you believed in his beloved Son, and not because of anything you have done. You enter through the door of faith into Jesus's grace where you now stand. You are surrounded by God's love and protection. Grace is when you receive the Father, Jesus Christ and the Holy Spirit into your heart. They will protect you from the evil within you.

Love and Joy

If you keep my commands, you will remain in my love, just as I have kept my Father's commands and remain in his love. I have told you this so that my joy may be in you and that your joy may be complete. John 15.10 and 11

The Holy Spirit

<u>If anyone loves me, he will obey my teaching. My Father will love him, and WE will come to him and make OUR home with him</u><u>. John 14.23</u>

This passage changed my life. It made me realise that to stay in Jesus' love, I had to obey his commands. And, secondly, it taught me that Jesus Christ, the Son of God, and God, the Father, lives in me through the Holy Spirit. Two revelations that changed my heart forever.

This is Jesus' promise of The Holy Spirit. By believing, you receive the gift of the Holy Spirit which is a life changing experience. He will be with you always guiding and helping you even when you do not know he is there. This statement implies that not only is the Holy Spirit in you, but God and Jesus are also in you through the Holy Spirit.

But note it is conditional there is an 'if'. To receive the Holy Spirit, you must Love Jesus and obey his teachings.

With it comes responsibility. If the Holy Spirit is in you, you don't want to upset or grieve the Holy Spirit that is in you. You want to do the opposite and please the Holy Spirit that is in you. You please the Holy Spirit in you by loving Jesus and obeying his teachings.

Do you not know that you are the temple of God, and that the Spirit of God dwells in you. 1 Cor. 3:16

If you love me, keep my commands. And I will ask the Father, and he will give you another Helper to help you and be with you forever - the Spirit of Truth. John 14.15 and 16

The Holy Spirit is with you forever.

Serve in the way of the Spirit.

You become part of the body of Christ and within that body you will have abilities that can be used to serve Jesus (gifts of the Spirit). If you don't know what your gift is then you need to ask God to show you. You receive the fruit of the Spirit. The fruit of the Spirit is love, peace, forbearance, kindness, goodness, faithfulness. Forbearance is defined as - patient, self-control, restraint and tolerance. Gentleness is not one of the fruits but is mentioned in Philippians 4.4 as a quality that you should have.

Eternal Life

Now this is eternal life: that they know you, the only true God, and to know Jesus Christ, whom you have sent. John 17.3

To know God read John 14, 15 and 17

Chapter 7 – To be Sorry for your Sins (Repentance).

God commands all people everywhere to repent. Acts 17.30

Repent, then, and turn to God, so that your sins may be wiped out, that times of refreshing may come from the Lord. Acts 3.19

Whoever believes in him is not condemned, but whoever does not believe stands condemned already because they have not believed in the Name of God's one and only Son. John 3.18-19

Sin is not to believe in Jesus (John 16.9). Non-believers stand condemned. Sin is not to believe and love God, but to put yourself before God. Sin is not to obey God's commands in the Old Testament and Jesus' commands in the New Testament.

Sin has forced a gap between God and Man

For all have sinned and fall short of the glory of God.
Romans 3.23

Jesus Bridges that Gap

**For Christ also suffered once for sins, the righteous
for the unrighteous, to bring you to God.** 1 Peter 3.18

If we confess our sins, he is faithful and just and will forgive us our sins and purify us from all unrighteousness. 1 John 1.9

Those whom I love, I rebuke and discipline. So be earnest and repent. Revelations 3.19

Repentance is about change. It is not only about being sorry for not obeying Jesus in the past, but also about trying with all your heart to obey all Jesus' commands in the future. Only the Holy Spirit in you, can help you truly repent your sins. The body and the mind are weak and will continue to sin. It is only the intercession of the Holy Spirit that can change you. Only God can deliver you from evil (last line of the Lord's prayer).

Repentance is the commitment to try and obey all Jesus' commands, not just the ones that suit you, with the help of the Holy Spirit within you. Repentance does not come from your strength, but the strength of the Holy Spirit in you.

Repentance is hard because you cannot undo the bad things you have done in the past. You need to be sorrowful for your old ways, but you cannot let them drag you down. You have got to leave your sins behind you. You need to forgive yourself. Each day you start with a clean sheet. Repentance is about looking forward not looking back. It is part of the healing process and comes after asking Jesus to come into your heart and before you are baptised.

Repentance is recognising that you are arrogant and self-centred. You can change yourself by humbling yourself before God. You humble yourself by giving him respect.

RESPECT GOD, THE FATHER, AND RESPECT JESUS CHRIST FOR WHAT THEY HAVE DONE FOR YOU.

Respect Jesus Christ, the Son of God, for the pain and suffering that he endured for you on the cross.

Surely, he took up our pain and bore our suffering, yet we considered him punished by God, stricken by him, and afflicted. But he was pierced for our transgressions, he was crushed for our iniquities; the punishment that brought us peace was on him, and by his wounds we are healed. Isaiah 53.4 - 5

Respect God, the Father, for the wonderful world he created for you.

He heals the broken-hearted and binds up their wounds. He determines the number of the stars and calls them each by name. Great is our Lord and mighty in power; his understanding has no limit. Psalm 147.3-5

He made the earth by his power; he founded the world by his wisdom and stretched out the heavens by his understanding. Jeremiah 51.15

Chapter 8 - Be Baptized

Repent and be baptized, every one of you, in the name of Jesus Christ for the forgiveness of your sins. And you will receive the gift of the Holy Spirit. Acts 2.38

No one can see the Kingdom of God unless they are born again. John 3.3

No one can enter the Kingdom of God unless they are born of water and the Spirit. John 3.5

Your baptism is an outward sign that you have died to your old self and are born anew in Jesus.

Although baptism in water is a once in a lifetime experience, your spirit can be born anew or refreshed each day. The Holy Spirit is in you teaching your spirit. Each day, you can ask the Holy Spirit in you to refresh your spirit, soul and mind.

Therefore, go and make disciples of all nations, baptizing them in the NAME of the Father and of the Son and of the Holy Spirit, and teaching them to obey everything I have commanded you. And surely, I am with you always, to the very end of the age. Matthew 28.19

You need to find a Christian living near you and ask him or her to baptize you. You need to find a river, lake, sea or a tub of water to be baptized in. Your Chistian friend should immerse you totally in the water saying the words: Because you believe in Jesus Christ, I baptize you in NAME of the Lord Jesus Christ.

Peter replied, Repent and be baptized, every one of you, in the NAME of Jesus Christ for the forgiveness of your sins. And you will receive the gift of the Holy Spirit. Acts 2.38

So do you baptize people in the NAME of the Father, Son and Holy Spirit or do you baptize them in the NAME of Jesus Christ?

I believe that in the early church, the disciples wanted to differentiate themselves from any other teachings other than Jesus Christ's teachings. The baptism symbolised the death of the old self with the death of Jesus (going under the water) and the birth of the new self in the resurrection of Jesus (coming up out of the water). They used the name Jesus Christ so everyone was in no doubt that Jesus Christ was the source of their salvation.

Chapter 9 - Love

Follow the way of love and eagerly desire spiritual gifts.
1 Corinthians 14.1

Paul encourages you to follow the way of love. God's love is in your heart. Love is described in 1 Corinthians 13 as follows:

**Love is patient,
Love is kind,
It does not envy,
It does not boast,
It is not proud,
It is not rude,
It is not self-seeking,
It is not easily angered,
It keeps no record of wrongs.
Love does not delight in evil
But rejoices with the truth.
It always protects,
Always trusts,
Always hopes,
Always perseveres.
Love never fails**.
1 Corinthians 13. 4

Since you believe in Jesus and have asked him into your life, you have Jesus' love in your heart. Your 'old' self is dead, and you are alive in Jesus. These are Jesus' qualities, and he wants you to show the same qualities.

Just reading these words or saying them in your mind brings an inner sense of calm.

In 1 Corinthians 13.10 it describes God's love as perfect. That means there are only four perfect things in the universe: God, Jesus Christ, the Holy Spirit and God's Love.

God's love is perfect and never fails. It perseveres and protects. **Love must be your motivation in everything you do**. Otherwise, everything you do is meaningless (1 Corinthians 13.1 to 3). You can speak in tongues, prophecies, have faith to move mountains, but if you do not have God's love in you, it is nothing.

God is everlasting, so God's love is everlasting. It also never fails. That's how powerful and gentle it is. Now this powerful and gentle love is in you. How magnificent is that. Paul says that following the way of love is a most excellent way to live.

If anyone loves me (Jesus), he will obey my teaching. My Father will love him, and WE will come to him and make OUR home with him. John 14.23

This passage from John's gospel shows that God's love goes around in a circle. You love Jesus and God loves you in return. The circular flow of love. You enter grace through faith in Jesus Christ and receive God's unconditional love. God loves you and asks you to love him in return. Hence there is a circular flow of love.

Little children, love one another
As your heavenly Father loves you.

Love keeps no records of wrongs. 1 Corinthians 13.5

Each day you start with a clean sheet. There is a clean
sheet for your sins and a clean sheet for the sins of all
those people that have sinned against you (because you
have forgiven them). Jesus' death on the cross has taken
them all away.

Although you are part of the world, you are different
from the world because Jesus' love is in your heart. This
changes your disposition to yourself and the people
around you. You now have a greater capacity to love
your family, friends and even your enemies.

**And hope does not put us to shame, because God's
love has been poured out into our hearts through the
Holy Spirit, who has been given to us**. Romans 5.5

God has poured his love into our hearts. We need to use
this love for His Glory and not let it go to waste. What
do we do with this love. We do five things:

We love God, the Father,
We love Jesus Christ, God's Son,
We love the people who are kind to us (parable of the
good Samaritan),

We love other Christians
We love our enemies.

Love should be the motivation for all that you do and feel. It is the oil in your lamp that shines for Jesus.

God is love. Whoever lives in love lives in God, and God in them. 1 John 4.16

So, if you follow the way of God's love, God will live in you through the Holy Spirit.

GOD'S LOVE - USE IT,
DO NOT ABUSE IT
USE IT FOR HIS GLORY

Jesus last words in his prayer to the Father for us: I have made you known to them, and will continue to make you known in order that the love you have for me may be in them and that I myself may be in them. John 17.26

Our hearts are full of God's pure love. The same love that he has for Jesus. How wonderful is that. WOW. You must use that love in your prayers. Like the story of the talents, you must give it back to God with interest.

Chapter 10 - Obedience

OBEYING JESUS WILL GIVE YOU ETERNAL LIFE BECAUSE BY OBEYING JESUS YOU WILL REMAIN IN HIS LOVE

Churches should have this in writing on their walls and they should teach it constantly.

If you obey my commands, you will remain in my love. John 15.10

This is a life changer. If you obey Jesus' commands, you will remain in Jesus' love. To remain in Jesus' love, you must obey Jesus commands.

If you do not obey Jesus commands, you do not remain in his love and like the branches on the vine that wither and die, you will be cut off (John 15.1).

Therefore, go and make disciples of all nations, baptizing them in the name of the Father and of the Son and of the Holy Spirit, and teaching them to obey everything I have commanded you. And surely, I am with you always, to the very end of the age. Matthew 28.19

These were the last words that Jesus spoke before ascending into heaven. He told his disciples to make us into disciples and to teach us OBEDIENCE to his commands.

His teachings on how you should behave are set out in the four gospels. A list of some of his commands is found in Matthew Chapters 5, 6 and 7 which are summarised at Annex 2. Each day try to obey his commands. You should have them in your heart and in your mind, helped by the Holy Spirit.

I tried with all my strength to obey Jesus's commands, but satan new my weaknesses and I always failed. Until I learned that obedience comes from the strength of the Holy Spirit inside me.

Obedience and humility are the keys to the Kingdom of Heaven.

If you love me (Jesus), you will obey what I command. John 14.15

Jesus asks us to obey his commands, as an outward demonstration that we love him.

If you keep my commands, you will remain in my love, just as I have kept my Father's commands and remain in his love. I have told you this so that my joy may be in you and that your joy may be complete. John 15. 10 -11

By keeping Jesus' commands, you will not only remain in his love, but you will share in his joy and your joy will be complete.

If you obey Jesus Christ's commands, your heart will be right with God.

Chapter 11 – Forgiveness

(Father) forgive us our debts, as we also have forgiven our debtors. Matthew 6.12

For if you forgive other people when they sin against you, your heavenly Father will also forgive you. But if you do not forgive others their sins, your Father will not forgive your sins. Matthew 6. 14

You must forgive everyone who has or will hurt or abuse you. This is fundamental to the cleansing of your heart. This will release you from the chains of the past that hold you down. Forgiveness comes from the heart (Matthew 18.35). In future, whenever the hurt or abuse comes to mind, your forgiveness will also come to mind. Your forgiveness will be with you, inside your heart, for the rest of your life. It is a continuous process. But you are not alone. Jesus' powerful and forgiving love is inside you, helping you. Jesus's love inside you keeps no record of wrongs. It perseveres, protects and never fails. Whatever you have done wrong, if you have forgiven others from your heart, God will forgive you. Your sins are wiped clean.

Love and forgiveness go hand in hand. If you love someone, you will also forgive them. If you forgive them, you will also love them.

Forgive from your heart.

Little children, forgive one another
As your heavenly Father forgives you.

And forgive yourself.

Forgiveness comes from the strength of the Holy Spirit
inside you.

Your forgiveness is every day as God's forgiveness to
you is every day. Forgiveness cleanses the soul.

Chapter 12– One Spirit, One Lord and One God

**There is one God, the Father, from whom all things
were made, and for whom we exist. and there is one
Lord, Jesus Christ, through whom all things were
made, and through whom we exist.** 1 Corinthians 8.6

   **There is one body, one Spirit, one Lord, one faith,
one hope, one baptism, one God and Father of all,
who is over all and through all and in all.** Ephesians
4.4

There is one Spirit, the Holy Spirit.

There is one Lord, Jesus Christ, the Son of God

There is one true God, the Father.

They are three separate persons.

If anyone loves me, he will obey my teaching. My Father will love him, and <u>WE</u> will come to him and make OUR home with him. John 14.23

When you receive the Holy Spirit, you also receive the Father and Jesus because they are ALWAYS PRESENT TOGETHER,

The three are separate persons, but they are always present together.

There is only one God, the Father

There is one Lord, Jesus Christ, the Son of God.

There is one Spirit – the Spirit of Truth.

BUT they are always present together.

The three persons have three different functions.

The Father's function is decision maker. It was he who decided to send Jesus into the world to save the world. It is he who will decide when the world comes to an end.

Jesus' function was to reveal the Father to the world and to save the world. He came from the Father and returned to the Father. His function now is to give us access to the

Father. You can only come to the Father through Jesus Christ. Jesus is the only way to God.

The Holy Spirit's function is to help us and to teach us the truth.

The Holy Spirit, Jesus and the Father are ALWAYS PRESENT TOGETHER. When the Holy Spirit is with you, so are the Father and Jesus. They are INSEPARABLE.

Believe me when I say that I am in the Father and he Father is in me. John 14.11

Jesus said that he was in the Father and the Father was in him (inseparable).

 We are in Jesus and Jesus is in God, so we are in God. And God and Jesus are in us.

Chapter 13 - Jesus is not God. Jesus is the Son of God

There is but one God, the Father, from whom all things came and for whom we live; and there is but one Lord, Jesus Christ, through whom all things came and through whom we live. 1 Corinthians 8.6

I believed for many years that Jesus should be worshiped as God because he was part of the Godhead as taught by the trinity doctrine. This believe is held by most

Christians. But there was a niggling doubt in my head even though I knew all the verses of scripture that supported this theory. Then one day, someone made a comment to my post on You Tube. Yes, God, the Father, is in Jesus and Jesus is in the Father, but that does not make Jesus, God. In the same way we are in Jesus and Jesus is in us, does not make us Jesus. As soon as I realized Jesus was the Son of God and was not God, all the jigsaw pieces fell into place.

John who was Jesus' best friend, in his letters in the gospel, emphasizes that Jesus is the Son of God and does not refer to Jesus as God. I investigate the verses in the New Testament that support Jesus's deity, and when you examine the word-by-word translation from the Greek, there is room to doubt the translations.

Now this is eternal life: that they know you (God, the Father), the one true God, and know Jesus Christ, whom you sent. John 17.3

I believe, that in your search for the truth, that you need to know the one true God and worship him only, so if you believe the above verse, you only worship God, the Father. You do not worship Jesus. This does not lessen the importance of our Lord and Savour Jesus Christ, through whom we have access to God and through whom we serve God in our daily lives. Apart from Jesus we can achieve nothing. The gospels say that believing that Jesus is the Son of God, is the only way to everlasting life.

There is no evidence from the letters of the apostles in the New Testament of the early Christians worshipping Jesus as God. It was only in the third century that Christians started believing that Jesus was God. And since then, many of the Bible translators have been influenced, consciously or subconsciously by this doctrine in how they have translated the original Greek and Hebrew manuscripts. It is because the evidence in the Old and New Testaments for Jesus being God is so questionable, the debate has gone on and on.

The evidence in the New Testament clearly supports Jesus Christ being the Son of God. God himself speaks twice to confirm this.

And a voice from heaven said, this is my Son, whom I love; with him I am well pleased. Matthew 3.17

While he was still speaking, a bright cloud covered them, and a voice from the cloud said, this is my Son, whom I love; with him I am well pleased. Listen to him. Matthew 17.5

God was proud of his son and loved him deeply. Now the love that God had for Jesus is in us who believe that Jesus is the Son of God.

I have made you known to them, and will continue to make you known in order that the love you have for me may be in them and that I myself may be in them. John 17.26

Most Christians belief that Jesus is God because they have been misled by bad translations of the bible. I believe that provided you accept Jesus as your Savior and keep Jesus' commands, your heart will right with God. If your heart is right with God, then you will be saved on judgement day.

Chapter 14 – The Holy Spirit

But the Advocate (the Helper), the Holy Spirit, whom the Father will send in my name, will teach you all things and will remind you of everything I have said to you. John 14.26

May the grace of the Lord Jesus Christ, and the love of God, and the fellowship of the Holy Spirit be with you all. 2 Corinthians 13.14

Therefore, go and make disciples of all nations, baptising them in the name of the Father and of the Son and of the Holy Spirit. Matthew 28.19

<u>Fellowship with the Holy Spirit</u>

Wherever you are, whatever you are doing, you are not alone. You have a faithful friend with you always – the Holy Spirit. Feel the Holy Spirit in your heart. He loves you and cares for you. He guides you and protects you. Everything you have achieved in your Christian life has been achieved through him. He deserves your love, respect and friendship, in return. In your quiet moment, remember to thank him.

How do you know that you have received the Holy Spirit into your heart?

The Holy Spirit's name is **Helper** and that is what he does. You know that you have received him when you see yourself grow spiritually through his strength and not your own. He gives you the ability to understand the scriptures. Suddenly the Word of God becomes alive and active in your heart. He gives you the capacity to believe more, to love more, to forgive more, to get angry less, to repent more and to obey more.

Thank you, Holy Spirit for being my friend and guiding me and helping me each day.

When Jesus commanded his disciples to baptise people, he told them to baptise people in the name of the Father and of the Son and of the Holy Spirit (Matthew 28.19). He wanted the Holy Spirit to be recognised as a separate person. Jesus wants the Holy Spirit to receive the respect he deserves.

The Holy Spirit is your best friend and helper.

You can only truly **understand** the Bible with the help of the Holy Spirit.
You can only truly **repent** with the help of the Holy Spirit.
You can only truly **love** with the help of the Holy Spirit.
You can only truly **obey** with the help of the Holy Spirit.

You can only truly **bear fruit** with the help of the Holy Spirit.

Chapter 15 - Bear Fruit

If a man remains in me and I in him, he will bear much fruit; apart from me you can do nothing. John 15.5

Jesus says that he is the vine, the Father is the gardener, we are the branches, and we should bear fruit. Bear fruit means telling people about Jesus. You tell them about Jesus, Jesus will turn them and heal their hearts.

If you remain in Jesus, you will bear much fruit. Like the good branches on the vine, God will prune you and care for you so that you bear much fruit. If you do not remain in Jesus, you will not bear fruit and you will be cut off.

There is a condition - you must remain in Jesus. How do you remain in Jesus? By obeying his commands.

If you remain in me and my words remain in you, ASK whatever you wish, and it will be done for you. This is to my Father's glory, that you bear much fruit, showing yourselves to be my disciples. John 15.7 and 8.

This is a life changer. How do you bear fruit? This verse says that you bear fruit by asking. By asking God in prayer to save someone that you have told about Jesus. As simple as that.

You were created to bring glory to God, the Father. You bring glory to God, the Father, by telling someone about Jesus and ASKING God to save them.

Step 1 - Telling someone about Jesus - bearing witness for Jesus. In this modern age, you can witness for Jesus, through social media. You can witness for Jesus to the people around you by the lifestyle you lead.

Step 2 - **ASK God to save them in prayer.**

This will only happen if you remain in Jesus by obeying his commands and his words remain in in you. Jesus' words must be in you. You should have Jesus' words in our hearts and minds daily. Whether by reading the New Testament or from memory. They must be part of you. God will show you the words that are important to you.

Always remember the purpose of all this is for the glory of God. You are helped by the Holy Spirit in you and around you. You have received God's grace which is the love he gives you. You have God's righteousness which is credited to you by faith. Most of all, you have God's love in you. You know from 1 Corinthians 13 that God's love never ever fails.

For the Son of Man came to seek and to save the lost. Luke 19.10

Jesus came to seek and find the lost. Jesus is no longer with us, so it is up to you to seek and find the lost through the Holy Spirit that is in you. God will show you how.

Our Father help me seek and find the lost so that they might believe and be saved.

Chapter 16 - The First Seven Steps

The first three steps are:

· Believe in Jesus
· Ask and receive Jesus into your heart
· Repent of your sins

The next four steps are:

· Be Baptised – renew or refresh your spirit
· Love – follow the way of God's love
· Obey – God's and Jesus commands
· Bear Fruit – tell people about Jesus

All of this is for the GLORY OF GOD

You can commit to these seven steps each day. You can pray that the people that you pray for commit to these steps.

Believing in Jesus is base one.
Asking Jesus into your heart is base two.
Receiving the Holy Spirit is base three.
Repenting and Baptism is a home run.

These are the seven steps to finding God's Kingdom on earth today.

Chapter 17 - Pray for the Kingdom

The New Testament asks you to pray to the Father in many places.

Ask and it will be given to you; seek and you will find, knock and the door will be opened to you. Matthew 7.7

Do not be anxious about anything, by prayer and petition, with thanksgiving, present your requests to God. Philippians 4.4

If you remain in me and my words remain in you, ask whatever you wish, and it will be done for you. This is to my Father's glory, that you bear much fruit, showing yourselves to be my disciples. John 15.7-8

Jesus commands you to pray. You should talk to God frequently throughout the day. In the bathroom in the morning, over breakfast, on the bus waiting for the bus, walking the dog, in the gym, waiting in the dentist, driving the car, lying in bed first thing in the morning and last thing at night.

Jesus commands you to pray in secret - No one must know when you pray or what you pray for. Not even your wife or husband. It's your secret with God.

What do you pray for? – You pray for the Kingdom. Your Kingdom come.

Your Kingdom come in people hearts. You pray for the people that God puts in your heart to pray for. They might be individuals, towns, cities, countries or nations.

You pray that God will come into their hearts and deliver them from evil. Use the Lord's prayer as a model for your prayers.

Pray with passion for the people that God's put in your hearts to pray for. Pray with love in your heart believing that it will happen. Persevere with your prayers for those persons until God removes those persons from your memory which might be never.

Remembering God's love is perfect and never fails. When you pray with love in your heart for the salvation of the people of this world, a powerful mesh or web of love forms. Your prayers will bear fruit and advance the

Kingdom of Heaven for the Glory of God. You pray for the Kingdom:

Our Father, your Kingdom come in my heart and in the hearts of the people I pray for. Amen

You pray to the Father, in the name of Jesus and through the Holy Spirit. The prayer for personal salvation is directly to Jesus because only Jesus can save you (see chapter 5).

Love in, love out. love in, love out.
Your heart is a conduit (pipe) for God's love.
It flows through your heart like a pipe.
Your heart spreads it like a fertiliser over all God's chosen people.
You spread it over the whole world by prayer.
You spread it near (your family) and afar (Christians you see on You Tube).
Making yourself a prayer warrior for Jesus.
Yes, warrior because you are fighting evil.
Remember, it is not your love that you are spreading.
IT IS GOD'S LOVE THAT YOU ARE SPREADING,

Every prayer to the one and only true God matters, because every prayer acknowledges that God exists. You have access to God through Jesus. Only through Jesus can you access the one and only true God. Prayers that try to access God and do not go through Jesus, are empty prayers and disappear nowhere.

Now this is eternal life: that they know you, the only true God, and know Jesus Christ, whom you sent.
John 17.3

All true prayers matter. Every single pray counts. Even when the prayer is not answered, it still counts.

Chapter 18 - Finding the Kingdom

Jesus told you to:

Seek first the Kingdom and its righteousness.
Matthew 6.33

In Matthew 6, Jesus told you not to worry about what you eat, drink or wear or any aspect of your life but first seek his Kingdom and his righteousness and all these things will be yours. You seek God's Kingdom with your heart. You should seek God's Kingdom and his righteousness each day. This chapter is about how you go about finding God's Kingdom each day.

The Kingdom of God is made up of God's people. If you believe in Jesus, you are part of his Kingdom. If you have received the Holy Spirit, the Kingdom of God is in you now. You could say that you have already found the Kingdom because it is in you. You keep God's Kingdom in your heart. You remain in God's Kingdom by obeying Jesus' commands.

Jesus told many parables to explain the Kingdom of God. These parables fall into two types. There were those that explained the future Kingdom that will be set in place when Jesus returns. For examples, the parable of the weeds and the wheat (Matthew 13.25), and the parable of the wise and foolish virgins (Matthew 25.1-13). The other type of parables is those that referred to the Kingdom of God that exists in the now.

The Kingdom of Heaven is like treasure hidden in a field. When a man found it, he hid it again, and then in his joy went and sold all he had and bought that field. Matthew 13.44

The man had to consciously **search** for the Kingdom because it was hidden. You must seek the Kingdom to find it. The man didn't have to wait until the resurrection to find it. He found the joy of finding the Kingdom of Heaven in the present world, in the now. The Kingdom of Heaven is in you now. Note that he gave all he had to buy it. Jesus requires total commitment. It becomes the most important thing in your life. The Kingdom of Heaven is in your hearts because that where God's love is.

Again, the Kingdom of Heaven is like a merchant looking for fine pearls. When he found one of great value, he went away and sold everything he had and bought it. Matthew 13.45

Again, the merchant is **searching** for the pearl and again he sells all he has, to buy it.

He told them another parable: The Kingdom of Heaven is like a mustard seed, which a man took and planted in his field. Though it is the smallest of all seeds, yet when it grows, it is the largest of garden plants and becomes a tree, so that the birds come and perch in its branches. Matthew 13.31

The Kingdom of Heaven is like yeast that a woman took and mixed into about sixty pounds of flour until it worked all through the dough. Matthew 13.33

You find the Kingdom of God by praying for it. Praying for it to come into your heart and into the hearts of the people you know. You are the mustard seed and your prayers will cause the Kingdom of Heaven to grow like the mustard seed. You are the yeast and your prayers will cause the Kingdom of Heaven to spread like the yeast.

If you place your self in the right place with God, God will use you for his Glory. Guided by the Holy Spirit, motivated by his Love, he will give you the opportunity to serve him. Jesus must be in you to achieve God's outcome.

Jesus was determined to teach us about the Kingdom of Heaven. Most of Jesus' parables are about the Kingdom. He wants everyone to enter the Kingdom of Heaven.

The Parable of the Sower

Then he told them many things in parables, saying: A
farmer went out to sow his seed. As he was scattering
the seed, some fell along the path, and the birds came
and ate it up. Some fell on rocky places, where it did
not have much soil. It sprang up quickly, because the
soil was shallow. But when the sun came up, the
plants were scorched, and they withered because they
had no root. Other seed fell among thorns, which
grew up and choked the plants. Still other seed fell
on good soil, where it produced a crop—a hundred,
sixty or thirty times what was sown. Whoever has
ears, let them hear. The disciples came to him and
asked, "Why do you speak to the people in
parables?" He replied, "Because the knowledge of
the secrets of the Kingdom of Heaven has been given
to you, but not to them. Otherwise, they might see
with their eyes, hear with their ears, understand with
their hearts and turn, and I would heal them.

Listen then to what the parable of the sower
means: When anyone hears the message about the
Kingdom and does not understand it, the evil one
comes and snatches away what was sown in their
heart. This is the seed sown along the path. The seed
falling on rocky ground refers to someone who hears
the word and at once receives it with joy. But since
they have no root, they last only a short time. When
trouble or persecution comes because of the word,
they quickly fall away. The seed falling among the
thorns refers to someone who hears the word, but the

worries of this life and the deceitfulness of wealth choke the word, making it unfruitful. But the seed falling on good soil refers to someone who hears the word and understands it. This is the one who produces a crop, yielding a hundred, sixty or thirty times what was sown. Matthew 13. 1 to 23

To bear fruit for Jesus, you must hear the word and understand it. You must understand the message about the Kingdom. Notice the things that can happen to prevent this happening: worrying about your life, the deceit of wealth, trouble or persecution because of the word or, simply, not understanding. Satan does not want you to understand the message about the Kingdom. God does.

Otherwise, they (the people) might see with their eyes, hear with their ears, understand with their hearts and turn, and I would heal them. Matthew13.15

The Kingdom of Heaven is God's people here on earth now. To enter God's Kingdom, you need to see with your eyes, hear with your ears and understand with your heart. Once you understand you need to turn. It says Jesus himself will heal you. That how important understanding the message is. You should want to understand the message more than anything else in the world. The Kingdom of Heaven should be the centre of your life.

Rejoicing in Heaven

In the same way, I tell you, there is rejoicing in the presence of the angels of God over one sinner who repents. Luke 15. 10

Like the prodigal son, who realised he had sinned against his father and against heaven, you need to turn, and the Father will welcome you with open arms. The stories of the lost sheep (Luke 15.4-7), the lost coin (Luke 8-10) and the lost son (Luke 15.11-32) say that there will be rejoicing in heaven when one, just one, person repents and turns to God. Like the story of the one in a hundred sheep, the Father does not want to lose anyone. He wants everyone to turn to Jesus for salvation. When you turn to God, Jesus will heal you. You need Jesus' healing hands in your life, every day of your life. He will heal your heart.

The Kingdom of Heaven has been forcefully advancing and forceful men lay hold on it. Matthew 11.12

You forcefully advance the Kingdom of Heaven by praying for it to come into people's hearts.

Chapter 19 - Humility

To enter or receive the Kingdom of God you must humble yourself before God like a child. Only the humble will enter the Kingdom of Heaven. You need to change your attitude towards God and become lowly, gentle, and humble in your heart, recognising Him for who he is and you for who you are.

Truly I say to you unless you change and become like children you will not enter the Kingdom of Heaven. Whoever makes themselves lowly like this child, will be the greatest in the Kingdom of Heaven. Matthew 18.3-4

Humility was lost in the Garden of Eden. Man is self-centred and has forgotten how to be humble before God. The Holy Spirit will teach you how to be humble before God.

You are a spec of sand in a vast desert. God is the Universe. This feeling is humility.

You are nothingness. God is the Universe. This feeling is humility.

Humility of heart and spirit and obedience to Jesus' commands are the keys to the Kingdom.

My sacrifice, O God, is a broken spirit; a broken and contrite heart that you, God, will not despise. Psalm 51.17

Come before God, the Father in prayer, with a broken spirit and a broken and contrite (repentant) heart each day. This is your starting position when talking to God.

Humble yourselves, therefore, under God's mighty hand, that he may lift you up in due time. Cast all your anxiety on him because he cares for you. 1 Peter 5.6 to 7

Repentance and Humility go hand in hand.

Repentance is recognising that you are arrogant and self-centred. You can change yourself by humbling yourself before God. You humble yourself by giving him respect.

RESPECT GOD AND RESPECT JESUS CHRIST FOR WHAT THEY HAVE DONE FOR YOU.

Chapter 20 – Spirit, Heart, Soul, Mind and Body

There is a spiritual man with heart and spirit inside you and there is your physical man with mind, soul and body.

Spiritual Man

The heart and spirit of an unsaved person is set on earthly desires and needs. When you ask Jesus into your life, your heart and spirit are transformed. God's love is poured into your heart. The Holy Spirit enters your heart. Jesus' words enter your heart, Your heart is healed. Your heart miraculously understands Jesus' message and is turned. This can occur instantly or over a period of years. Your heart fills up with God's love and treasures leaving less room for earthly desires. Your heart's capacity to believe, love and obey is increased.

Because you are sons, God has sent forth the Spirit of His Son into your hearts, crying, "Abba! Father!" Galatians 4.6

And hope does not put us to shame, because God's love has been poured out into our hearts through the Holy Spirit, who has been given to us. Romans 5:5

Your heart is your innermost spiritual being. The heart thinks, plans and feels all your emotions.

Your heart is **fused** with your spirit because it is working continually with your spirit.

The spirit of an unsaved person is virtually dormant and inactive because they have no or little communication with God.

When you are saved the spirit is reborn, refreshed and made new (regeneration). Before you were an empty glass now you are full or partly filled glass.

The Holy Spirit that dwells in your heart combines with your new-born spirit to glorify and worship God. Your heart and spirit work together to serve and communicate with God.

The Spirit himself testifies with our spirit that we are God's children. Romans 8:16

This is the spiritual man that lives within the physical man.

<u>Physical Man</u>

The thoughts and deeds and emotions of your spiritual man **overflow** into the life of your physical man influencing your mind, soul and body. Goodness **overflows** from the heart into the soul.

For example, when you glorify God with your heart and spirit, this **overflows** into your mind, soul and body who also glorify God. If your heart is right with God, your soul and mind will follow because the soul and mind are led by the heart.

Love the Lord your God with all your heart and with all your soul and with all your mind and with all your strength. Mark 12.30

Your heart loves first and your soul and mind follow.

Unfortunately, not only does the good things overflow from your heart into your soul but also sinful thoughts and deeds. How do we stop these sinful thoughts when they occur in your heart and soul? Think or speak Jesus words when the thought occurs. God has given you his words in your hearts. Use these words to overcome the evil that is in you. I receipt, "Jesus said, I am the way, the truth and the life no one comes to the Father except through me" (John 14.6), or "The eyes are the light of the body, if eyes are good the whole body is good" (Matthew 6.22) also works for me.

The good man brings good things out of the good stored up in his heart, and the evil man brings evil things out of the evil stored up in his heart. For out of the OVERFLOW of his heart, his mouth speaks. Luke 6:45

When you die your spiritual body will go back to heaven. Your physical body will burn or rot away. However, at the resurrection, your soul will rise to meet the Lord and find rest in heaven. All the unsaved souls will suffer in hell. You are not alone. Your spiritual body is part of Jesus' spiritual body. Jesus said, remain in me and I will remain in you. You are part of the larger body of Christ.

Chapter 21 – Your Heart.

God's love has been poured out into our hearts through the Holy Spirit, who has been given to us. Romans 5:5

This is an amazing statement. God has poured his love into your heart. Is that amazing? Your old un-imaginative heart as now been filled with God's love increasing your capacity to love your family, friends and everyone else. He wants you to use that love, first, to love him (Matthew 22.37) and secondly, love everyone else (Matthew 22.39).

Not only is God's love in your heart but the Holy Spirit is also in your heart.

Because you are sons, God has sent forth the Spirit of His Son into our hearts, crying, "Abba! Father!" Galatians 4.6

If you think your heart is pretty full with the Holy Spirit and God's love in it, there is more. It is in your heart that you keep Jesus' words (Rev1.3 and Psalm 119.9). Your heart is where the Kingdom of Heaven is in you.

Your heart is the centre of your whole being. It is where you store all your heavenly treasure given to you by God. The treasure therein is your love for Jesus your Saviour, your love for the Father God Almighty, and your love for the Holy Spirit in you and around you.

Your heart is where you commit your life to God. Your heart is where you decide to follow Jesus.

Functions of the Heart.

It is with your heart that you believe. Faith comes from your heart.

If you declare with your mouth, "Jesus is Lord," and believe in your heart that God raised him from the

dead, you will be saved. For it is with your heart that you believe and are justified, and it is with your mouth that you profess your faith and are saved. Romans 10.9-10

It is with your heart that you love God.

Love the Lord your God with all your heart and with all your soul and with all your mind and with all your strength.
Mark 12.30

It is with your heart that you understand what is written in the Bible. You take God's words to heart.

Otherwise they (the people) might see with their eyes, hear with their ears, understand with their hearts and turn, and I would heal them. Matthew 13.15

You think with your heart.

For the word of God is alive and active. Sharper than any double-edged sword, it penetrates even to dividing soul and spirit, joints and marrow; it judges the thoughts and attitudes of the heart. Hebrews 4:12

You praise God with your heart.

I will praise you, Lord my God, with all my heart; I will glorify your name forever. Psalm 86:12

It is with the heart that you repent.

My sacrifice, O God, is a broken spirit; a broken and contrite (repentant) heart that you, God, will not despise. Psalm 51:17

You sing with your heart.

speaking to one another with psalms, hymns, and songs from the Spirit. Sing and make music from your heart to the Lord. Ephesians 5:19

You call on the Lord with your heart.

Flee the evil desires of youth and pursue righteousness, faith, love and peace, along with those who call on the Lord out of a pure heart. 2 Timothy 2:22

Your heart has a dark side. Both good and evil thoughts come from your heart.

For it is from within, out of a person's heart, that evil thoughts come—sexual immorality, theft, murder, adultery, greed, malice, deceit, lewdness, envy, slander, arrogance and folly. All these evils come from inside and defile a person. Mark 7.21-23

The good man brings good things out of the good stored up in his heart, and the evil man brings evil things out of the evil stored up in his heart. For out of the overflow of his heart his mouth speaks. (Luke 6:45).

The emotional state of your heart affects the rest of you.

A happy heart makes the face cheerful, but heartache crushes the spirit. Proverbs 15.13

a cheerful heart is good medicine, but a crushed spirit dries up the bones. Proverbs 17.22

The heart and spirit are fused together. The heart is the centre of your character. Your heart is closely linked to your spirit.

God has given you a new heart.

I will give them an undivided heart and put a new spirit in them; I will remove from them their heart of stone and give them a heart of flesh. Ezekiel 11:19

Rid yourselves of all the offences you have committed and get a new heart and a new spirit. Why will you die, people of Israel? Ezekiel 18:31

He has purified your heart by faith.

Let us draw near to God with a sincere heart and with the full assurance that faith brings, having our hearts sprinkled to cleanse us from a guilty conscience and having our bodies washed with pure water. Hebrews 10.22

God, who knows the heart, showed that he accepted them by giving the Holy Spirit to them, just as he did to us He did not discriminate between us and them, for he purified their hearts by faith. Acts 15.8-9.

At the time of judgement, God will judge your heart. The word of God judges your heart.

In the time of judgment God will expose the hidden counsels of the heart. 1 Corinthians 4.5

If you obey Jesus Christ's commands, your heart will be right with God.

Chapter 22 - Your Spirit

God, whom I serve in my spirit in preaching the gospel of his Son, is my witness how constantly I remember you. Romans 1.9

You serve God with your spirit.

When a baby is born, he has a spirit in him giving him life. As the body grows, the spirit grows in the same way until a fully-grown spirit exists in that person. But that spirit is inadequate or insufficient on its own. That is why there is no true happiness on earth. That spirit needs God's Holy Spirit to make it complete. People are walking about like half-filled glasses. Only when you receive the Holy Spirit inside you will your glass be topped up and become full (regeneration).

The Spirit himself testifies with our spirit that we are God's children. Romans 8.16

The Holy Spirit needs a conduit or vessel to serve God on earth. You are that conduit. The Holy Spirit combines with your spirit to pray, praise, worship and serve God. The most important thing your spirit does is serve and worship God. When you praise, worship and pray to God, the action starts in your spiritual man (heart and spirit) and **overflows** to your physical man (mind, body and soul).

I will pray with my spirit, but I will also pray with my mind; I will sing with my spirit, but I will also sing with my mind. 1 Corinthians 14:15

Your heart and spirit should be: destitute, steadfast, gentle, lowly, quiet and needing God. Jesus described his own heart as meek and lowly (Matthew 11.29)

And he began to teach them. He said: Blessed are the poor (destitute) in spirit, for theirs is the Kingdom of heaven. Matthew 5.1

Blessed are you when you realise that your spirit is insufficient or inadequate and need God's help. When you realise this, you will have found the Kingdom of Heaven

God encourages you to have a steadfast spirit.

Create in me a pure heart, O God, and renew a steadfast spirit within me. Psalm 51:10

(Steadfast means resolute and unwavering).

God encourages you to develop a quiet and gentle spirit.

Rather, it should be that of your inner self, the unfading beauty of a gentle and quiet spirit, which is of great worth in God's sight. 1 Peter 3:4

Your emotions

Your spirit is fused into the core of your heart and it is here that you feel your deepest emotions. These are the emotions that affect your daily disposition.

Your spirit is not constant. It varies with your moods and can be refreshed.

For they refreshed my spirit and yours also. Such men deserve recognition. 1 Corinthians 16:18

Your feelings are felt by your spirit.

When Jesus saw her weeping, and the Jews who had come along with her also weeping, he was deeply moved in spirit and troubled. John 11:33

Your perception comes from your spirit

 Immediately Jesus knew in his spirit that this was what they were thinking in their hearts, and he said to them, "Why are you thinking these things? Mark 2:8

Your spirit need the Lord and needs his grace.

The Lord be with your spirit. Grace be with you all. 2 Timothy 4:22

The grace of the Lord Jesus Christ be with your spirit. Amen.
Philippians 4:23

Your spirit gives your body life. You will give up your spirit when you die.

And when Jesus had cried out again in a loud voice, he gave up his spirit. Matthew 27.50

Purification

You need to ask God to purify both the spiritual man (spirit) and the physical man (body) in you.

Therefore, since we have these promises, dear friends, let us purify ourselves from everything that contaminates body and spirit, perfecting holiness out of reverence for God. 2 Corinthians 7:1

May God himself, the God of peace, sanctify you through and through. May your whole spirit, soul and body be kept blameless at the coming of our Lord Jesus Christ. 1 Thessalonians 5:23

Chapter 23 - Your Soul

The feelings, emotions and thoughts of your heart overflow into your soul. Your soul is led by your heart. If your heart is good your soul will follow.

God will judge the words and thoughts of your heart, but if your heart is found wanting, it is your soul that will pay the price of sin.

Do not be afraid of those who kill the body but cannot kill the soul. Rather, be afraid of the One who can destroy both soul and body in hell. Matthew 10:28

What good is it for someone to gain the whole world, yet forfeit their soul? Mark 8:36

The soul of sinful man will be destroyed in hell. This is what satan wants.

The soul is part of physical man which consists of soul, mind and body. The spirit is part of spiritual man consisting of heart and spirit. Jesus' words are part of spiritual man and **overflow** from the spirit to the soul at times of worship. Hence the word of God divides soul and spirit.

For the word of God is alive and active. Sharper than any double-edged sword, it penetrates even to dividing soul and spirit, joints and marrow; it judges the thoughts and attitudes of the heart. Hebrews 4:12

You need to ask God to sanctify both your spiritual man (spirit) and your physical man (soul and body). Both need to be kept blameless. But if the heart and spirit are right with God, the soul will follow.

May God himself, the God of peace, sanctify you through and through. May your whole spirit, soul and body be kept blameless at the coming of our Lord Jesus Christ. 1 Thessalonians 5:23

Seeking God's Kingdom and righteousness each day of your life will keep your heart pure. A pure heart will lead to a pure soul that praises the Lord each day.

Dear friends, I urge you, as foreigners and exiles, to abstain from sinful desires, which wage war against your soul. 1 Peter 2:11

Praise the LORD, my soul; all my inmost being, praise his holy name. Psalm 103:1

Your forgiveness is every day as God's forgiveness to you is every day. Forgiveness cleanses the soul.

Jesus gives rest to your soul. He said:

Come to me, all you who are weary and burdened, and I will give you rest. Take my yoke upon you and learn from me, for I am gentle and humble in heart, and <u>you will find rest for your soul</u>. For my yoke is easy and my burden is light. Matthew 11.28 to 30

Jesus will restore your soul after it has been battered by the worries of your life:

The LORD is my shepherd, I shall not want. He makes me lie down in green pastures, he leads me beside quiet waters, <u>He restores my soul.</u> He leads me in paths of righteousness for his Name's sake. Even though I walk through the valley of the shadow of death, I will fear no evil, for you are with me; your rod and your staff, they comfort me. You prepare a table before me in the presence of my enemies. You anoint my head with oil; my cup overflows. Surely your goodness and mercy will follow me all the days of my life, and I will dwell in the house of the LORD forever. Psalm 23

The LORD, your God commands you this day to follow these decrees and laws; carefully observe them

with all your heart and with all your soul.
Deuteronomy 26.16

The law of the LORD is perfect, refreshing the soul. The statutes of the LORD can be trusted, making simple people wise. Psalm 19.7

The soul is the mirror image of the heart. What the heart thinks and does the soul follows. The heart is part of spiritual man the soul is part of physical man. God's words are stored in your heart but when you think of them, they restore, refresh and revive the soul.

Then he said to them, my soul is overwhelmed with sorrow to the point of death. Stay here and keep watch with me. Matthew 26.38

When your physical body dies the soul dies too, only to be revived on judgement day. The soul dies but your spirit returns to God.

Chapter 24 – Obey Jesus' Commands.

If you obey my commands, you will remain in my love
John 15.10

To stay in Jesus' commands, you must obey his commands.

Love the Lord your God with all your heart and with all your soul and with all your mind and with all your strength.
Mark 12.30

This is Jesus' greatest command. Notice that you not only love with your heart, but also you love with your soul and mind. If you love someone with your heart, soul and mind you really are loving them. It shows the circular flow of love. If we love God, God will love us in return.

And the second is like it: Love your neighbour as yourself.
Matthew 22.39

Jesus' teachings on how you should behave, are set out in Matthew 5, 6 and 7. It is very important that you live each day in accordance to Matthew 5,6 and 7. That is what Jesus wants you to do. He wants you to follow these commands.

Matthew Chapter 5

Chapter 5 covers Jesus' sermon on the mount in which he tells all the people how they should behave. Before the sermon Jesus preached to the people, 'Repent for the Kingdom of heaven is near' – Matthew 4.17. Becoming a Christian is a life changing experience and not to be entered lightly. As part of the change, God expects you to acknowledge that your old life was wrong. It might not feel that wrong, but because you did not love God and believe in Jesus before, your old life was sinful.

The Beatitudes

Jesus starts by explaining how you (heart, spirit and mind) should be towards God (the beatitudes).

And he began to teach them. He said:
Blessed are the poor (destitute) in spirit, for theirs is the Kingdom of heaven.
Blessed are those who mourn, for they will be comforted.
Blessed are the meek, for they will inherit the earth.
Blessed are those who hunger and thirst for righteousness, for they will be filled.
Blessed are the merciful, for they will be shown mercy.
Blessed are the pure in heart, for they will see God.
Blessed are the peacemakers, for they will be called children of God.
Blessed are those who are persecuted because of righteousness, for theirs is the Kingdom of heaven.
Matthew 5.1 to 14

These are the 8 conditions of heart and mind to please God.

The poor in spirit - Your spirit is poor because you realise how inadequate your life is and how much you need God. Your spirit concedes to God.

Those that mourn – Those who pray for God's help. How do you mourn? You mourn by praying to God either for yourself or other people. The Holy Spirit is the comforter. You should mourn to God for help each day.

Happy are the meek - They that are humble before God. Humility is the key to the Kingdom of Heaven. Your heart and spirit must be meek and humble to enter the Kingdom of Heaven.

They that hunger and thirst after righteousness - Those who want to be right with God. Righteousness is achieved through faith. You should seek righteousness every day of your life.

The merciful are those that forgive when they have the power to punish or hurt. You should forgive the people around you and not hurt or punish them by what you say or do.

The pure in heart – your heart is made pure by God's love. You keep it pure by obeying Jesus' commands and by abstains or avoiding things of the world that might corrupt your heart.

The peace makers – Those that spread the word of Christ. The Sowers of the word who keep Jesus' words in their hearts. At the right opportunity, tell people that you believe in Jesus.

You are persecuted when someone says, thinks or does bad things against you because you are a Christian. This is a situation you find you self in through no fault of your own. Don't worry because God's love will protect you. Endure dislike because God's love is with you.

Jesus starts by explaining how you (heart, spirit and mind) should be towards God (the beatitudes). The world will not understand them but we as Christians need to understand them. If you follow them then you are following Jesus' way - to remain in his love.

If you obey my commands, you will remain in my love
John 15.10

You are the salt of the earth. But if the salt loses its saltiness, how can it be made salty again? It is no longer good for anything, except to be thrown out and trampled underfoot.
Matthew 5.13

Although we Christians are few in numbers, we put God's flavour into the whole world. But be careful, because if you do not obey Jesus commands, you can fall out of Jesus' love and lose your saltiness and be worthless (Similar to the dead branches on the vine (John 15).

You are the light of the world. A town built on a hill cannot be hidden. Neither do people light a lamp and put it under a bowl. Instead, they put it on its stand, and it gives light to everyone in the house. In the same way, let your light shine before others, that they may see your good deeds and glorify your Father in heaven.
Matthew 5.14 to 16

When Jesus was in the world, he was the light of the world. When he left, we became the light of the world. Let your light shine so everyone can see it. How do you shine your light? By the gentleness, patients and kindness you show when you do good things for others. You are justified by faith, but works are important so that your light can shine. This was one of Jesus' commands to you, Let your light shine.

Do not think that I (Jesus) have come to abolish the Law or the Prophets; I have not come to abolish them but to fulfil them. Matthew 5. 17

But whoever practices and teaches these commands (the old law) will be called great in the Kingdom of heaven. Matthew 5.19

Do not forget to keep the ten commandments. They are equally as important as Jesus' teachings.

Have only one God me
Do not worship idols.
Do not miss-use my name.
Rest for one day each week
Honour your father and your mother.
Do not murder.
Do not commit adultery.
Do not steal.
Do not lie.
Do not covet.

They are just as important in today's world as they were in biblical times.

Jesus added the following 6 commands to these ten. This is a summary of Mathew 5. 21 to 48.

Do not be angry, be friends with everyone.

Do not look at a woman lustfully.

Do not divorce your wife unless she is unfaithful.

Keep your promises, keeping them simple as yes or no.

Do not resist an evil person who hurts you or steals from you.

Love and pray for your enemies and those who dislike you.

Matthew Chapter 6.

Give to the needy in secret.
Fast in secret
Pray in secret.
And your Father will reward you.
(Summary of Matthew 6. 1 to 18)

Jesus emphasised the importance of doing all these in secret.
As far as possible, you should do them without telling your
wife, your children, your family. The Lord will give you the
opportunity to do them in secret,

Jesus taught you how to pray:

Our Father who art in heaven
Hallowed is your name (YAHWEH)
Your Kingdom come.
Your will be done on earth as it is in heaven.
Give us today our daily bread.
And forgive us our trespasses.
As we forgive others their trespasses against us
And lead us not into temptation.
But deliver us from evil. Matthew 6. 9 to 13

You should pray to the Father. His name is important, and it
is YAWEH. You should pray for the Kingdom. The Kingdom of
God is made up of the people of God. The Kingdom of God is
in your hearts. You should therefore pray for the Kingdom of
God to come into people's hearts. God will lay on your heart
the people., the towns, the countries and the nations that he
wants you to pray for.

Heavenly Father, You are a holy and righteous God. I pray for your people all over the world. Please Father, send the Holy Spirit into their hearts so that they will believe in Jesus Christ and keep his commands. Amen
.

Ask God's help to deliver you and the rest of the world from evil each day. The enemy is in you and around you. You should ask for God's help each day.

Use the Lord's prayer as a model for your prayers.

Forgiving others is so important it is mentioned twice.

For if you forgive other people when they sin against you, your heavenly Father will also forgive you. Matthew 6. 14

Forgiving - Letting go of the past. Letting go of things that hold you. Setting yourself free from the past. Forgiveness is continuous. It is not a onetime thing. That is why Jesus asks us to do it daily in the Lord's prayer.

But there is a bonus. If you forgive others in your heart, God will forgive you your sins. Each day you start with a clean sheet holding no resentment for anyone or anything. You will feel a lightness in your heart as God's love takes over.

Fasting

Fasting. In Matthew 6 it says when you fast not if you fast. So why do you fast? It is explained in Acts 13. 1 to 3. You fast to show God that you are serious about what you are praying for and that you are intent on those prayers being answered. Fasting intensifies your prayers. Fasting makes your prayers stronger.

Treasures in Heaven

But store up for yourselves treasures in heaven, where moths and vermin do not destroy, and where thieves do not break in and steal. For where your treasure is, there your heart will be also. Matthew 6. 20 -22

This section comes immediately after Jesus tells you that God will reward you if you give to the needy, pray and fast in secret. Doing these things will result in you being rewarded. It does not just say store it says store up. That means the more you do these activities the more rewards that will accumulate.   This is our heavenly treasure which is unlike any earthly treasure.

Your body might belong to the world, but your heart belongs to Jesus. Your heart is part of God's heavenly Kingdom. Your heart is in the Kingdom of Heaven that is in you. Your heart is where Jesus' love remains. His love combined with your love creates a love that never fails.

Your heart must be right when you give, pray and fast.
Give to the needy with love.
Pray for others with love.
Fast with love.

The Eye

The eye is the lamp of the body. If your eyes are healthy, your whole body will be full of light. But if your eyes are unhealthy, your whole body will be full of darkness.
Matthew 6. 22

If Jesus's love is in you, you will look at life with a completely different attitude. You will see with your heart the goodness and beauty that is in the world that he created.

Human nature makes you lust, covet and envy. Jesus' love overcomes these desires and helps you see with a healthy attitude.

You can train your eyes to be good so that when you feel human nature taking control of your mind, YOU THINK OF JESUS' WORDS. Reciting Jesus' words will expel any bad thoughts from your head.

You cannot serve both God and money. Matthew 6. 24

Jesus tells you to serve God. You were created to serve God. There is no choice. When you serve God, you trust in Him and He will provide. You serve God by believing in Jesus and obeying his commands.

Everybody needs money to live. Money is hard to earn. You spend most of our waking life earning it. But it is wrong when money controls your life. God should be the motivation for all you do. You should not be motivated by money.

Worry

Therefore, I tell you, do not worry about your life, what you will eat or drink; or about your body, what you will wear. Is not life more than food, and the body more than clothes...
But seek first his Kingdom and his righteousness, and all these things will be given to you as well. Matthew 6. 25 and 33

This a wonderful command. Do not worry about anything. He knows that our human nature is to worry, and He tells you to stop it immediately and start trusting in God every day of your life. Now you have stopped worrying, what do you do instead each day. Each day you seek his Kingdom and his righteousness. How do you do this by praying for the Kingdom.

Matthew Chapter 7

Judgement

Do not judge, or you too will be judged. Matthew 7.1

As soon as you see a person, your human nature has formed an opinion of that person. That is human nature and very difficult to stop. The eyes are the lamp of the body and if the eyes are good the whole body is good (Matthew 6.22). If Jesus's love is in you and your eyes are good, you will not be judgemental.

Do not give dogs what is sacred; do not throw your pearls to pigs. If you do, they may trample them under their feet, and turn and tear you to pieces. Matthew 7.6

You should be friendly towards others, yet cautious of their human nature. Be discreet with whom you share your inner beliefs. The Holy Spirit will guide you as to whom to witness. You don't witness to everybody.

Asking

Ask and it will be given to you; seek and you will find; knock and the door will be opened to you. Matthew 7.7

Jesus commands you to ASK (A= ask, S = seek, K = knock). God wants you to ask for things. He wants you to communicate with him each day.

Evil in Us

If you, then, though you are evil, know how to give good gifts to your children, how much more will your Father in heaven give good gifts to those who ask him. Matthew 7.11

This is Jesus stating as a fact that you are evil because your human nature was corrupted by satan in the Garden of Eden. It is good and sobering to remember that you are indeed evil, and you are completely reliant on God for your salvation from the evil in you.

Enter through the narrow gate. For wide is the gate and broad is the road that leads to destruction, and many enter

through it. But small is the gate and narrow the road that leads to life, and only a few find it. Matthew 7.13 -14

Watch out for false prophets. Thus, by their fruit you will recognise them. Matthew 7.15 and 20

Not everyone who says to me, 'Lord, Lord,' will enter the Kingdom of heaven, but only the one who does the will of my Father who is in heaven. Matthew 7.21

Everyone who hears these words of mine and puts them into practice is like a wise man who built his house on the rock. Matthew 7.24

At the end of his speech on how you should behave, Jesus said that whoever hears these words and, importantly, puts them into practice is like a wise man building his house on rocky hard foundations. You must do three things; hear the words, understand them and thirdly put them into practice in your daily lives.

It is not easy to obey all these commands. You will fail. Otherwise, you would be free of sin and nobody is free of sin. But what Jesus wants you to do is to try each day. But you are not on your own. You have the Holy Spirit inside you and God's love helping you each day.

Chapter 25 – Jesus is The Truth

Jesus answered, "I am the way and the truth and the life. No one comes to the Father except through me. Matthew 14.6

We live in the most confusing age. There are so many false beliefs and doctoring, so much false news and propaganda, so many lies and deceit because everyone is pushing their own agenda. There are so many people putting themselves before God.

Jesus is the Truth. When you say those words, you get the feeling of God's power in the room. While writing this book, a Voice spoke to me saying:

Truth and justice come through
Jesus our Lord and Saviour.
On this Jesus will build his church.
And the truth that is in you
Will set you free
From the sin that is in the world.
Stand in Jesus' faith and grace
Rejoice in his love.
Believe in him and anything is possible.

Jesus is the truth
And that truth reigns within your heart.

To the Jews who had believed him, Jesus said, If you hold to my teaching, you are really my

disciples. Then you will know the truth, and the truth will set you free. John 8.31-32

Chapter 26 - The Word of God

For the Word of God is alive and active. Sharper than any double-edged sword, it penetrates even to dividing soul and spirit, joints and marrow; it judges the thoughts and attitudes of the heart. Hebrews 4:12

The Word of God is not just words written in the Bible but is alive and active. These words have been poured into your heart through the Holy Spirit and in your heart they are alive and active.

If you remain in me and my words remain in you, ask whatever you wish, and it will be done for you. This is to my Father's glory, that you bear much fruit, showing yourselves to be my disciples. John 15.7 and 8.

In your heart, these words have power, and the Holy Spirit will teach you how to use that power.

First, Jesus' words are a defence from the evil one. Whenever you are tempted by receipting Jesus words you can overcome this temptation.

Secondly, if Jesus' words are in your heart, you can ask God for things to happen and provided those wishes are for God's glory and for the glory of His Kingdom, they will happen. You might not see them happen, but they will happen.

Thirdly, when you witness for Jesus, the Holy Spirit will teach you to use Jesus' words as a basis for what you say. Jesus' words are the basis of your life in Jesus, so when you speak the truth from your heart, his words will come out in some shape or form.

Fourthly, if Jesus' words are in your heart, you are sanctified (made holy).

Jesus words were not just Jesus' words. They were God's words and God's instructions to us. Jesus is the Word of God.

You are already clean because of the word I have spoken to you. John 15.3

When Jesus prayed to the Father for his disciples, he said.

Sanctify them (his disciples) by the truth; your word is truth. John 17.17

God's word is truth, and that truth sanctifies you.

So, when you read the Bible, God, through the Holy

Spirit, will help you understand the words so that they are no longer just words on paper, but meaningful words written on your heart.

Ask God to teach you how to use that power - the Power of His Words.

Chapter 27 - The Chosen

God has chosen you.

You chose God out of your own free will. But God knew that you would choose Him before you chose Him because He knows everything.

To God's elect, ... who have been chosen according to the foreknowledge of God the Father, through the sanctifying work of the Spirit, to be obedient to Jesus Christ and sprinkled with his blood: Grace and peace be yours in abundance. 1 Peter 1-2

For you (God, the Father) granted him (Jesus Christ) authority over all people that he might give eternal life to all those you have given him. John 17.2

God chose you before you were born and gave you to Jesus Christ to serve him. How wonderful is that.

You start your Christian adventure at the point, that you see with your eyes, hear with your ears, understand with

your heart and turn to Jesus. Jesus comes into your heart
and heals it. You understand with your heart and believe.
You receive the Holy Spirit, and your heart and spirit are
renewed. You are saved. You now stand in Jesus' grace.
You are righteous with God through your faith.

At this point, in Christian terms you are like a young
child (even though you are a grown person) who has
much to learn from Jesus. God has a long and fruitful
education planned for you.

At this point you have a split heart. Part of it holds the
Holy Spirit and God's love in you. Part of it holds your
sinful nature and desires. These two parts are in conflict
within you. This is the hybrid Christian struggling
between sin and goodness.

God has started a transformation process in you and
gradually or suddenly he turns your heart from being
self-seeking to being God seeking.   Your 'good' heart
becomes stronger, and God teaches you to use the power
of God's word to overcome your sinful desires. The
Kingdom of God grows in you. Each day you seek his
Kingdom and his righteousness, and the Holy Spirit
helps you.

Your life becomes controlled by the spiritual man (heart
and spirit) that lives inside you. Physical man (soul,
mind and body) has less control over your daily life.

The next change point comes when you dedicate
yourself completely to God and to his Glory. You give

him your heart, spirit, soul mind and body to serve him as He pleases. At this point, you completely trust in Jesus your Saviour and in God the Father Almighty. You are His.

This process took me 34 years. I am sure it can happen in days. Once you enter this wonderful state with God, anything can happen. Each day you live for Him and for his Glory.

May God himself, the God of peace, sanctify you through and through. May your whole spirit, soul and body be kept blameless at the coming of our Lord Jesus Christ. 1 Thessalonians 5.23

Chapter 28 - Jesus' Grace is Sufficient

Therefore, in order to keep me (Paul) from becoming conceited, I was given a thorn in my flesh, a messenger of Satan, to torment me. Three times I pleaded with the Lord to take it away from me. But he said to me, "My grace is sufficient for you, for my power is made perfect in weakness." Therefore, I will boast all the more gladly about my weaknesses, so that Christ's power may rest on me. That is why, for Christ's sake, I delight in weaknesses, in insults, in hardships, in persecutions, in difficulties. For when I am weak, then I am strong. 2 Corinthians 12. 7 to 10.

I knew that Grace is Jesus's love for those who believe, but until the Holy Spirit revealed these verses to me, I did not understand the significance of it.

Once you realise Jesus' grace is sufficient and grace is all you need to take on everything satan and the world throws at you. You then stand in Jesus' strength not your own. Insults, hardships, persecution, difficulties and physical weaknesses – bring them on. You will quietly, calmly thrive in these conditions because you have God's love in your heart, Jesus' grace in your heart and the friendship of the Holy Spirit in your heart.

Jesus said, I am the vine; you are the branches. If you remain in me and I in you, you will bear much fruit; apart from me you can do nothing. John 15.5

Jesus said that apart from him you can do nothing. So everything you do, should be in the strength of Jesus and the Holy Spirit and not in your own strength.

Grace is when you receive the Father, Jesus Christ and the Holy Spirit into your heart. They will protect you from the evil within you.

Chapter 29 - God's Will

Jesus explained to us what God's will is when he taught us the Lord's Prayer.

This, then, is how you should pray: Our Father in heaven, hallowed be your name, your kingdom come, your will be done, on earth as it is in heaven. Matthew 6. 9-10

God wants three things to happen:

1. **His Name** (Yahweh) is hallowed, respected, feared, loved, worshipped and glorified by you and all his chosen people.

2. **His Kingdom** comes into your heart and into the hearts of all his chosen people.

3. **His Will** is obeyed by you and all his chosen people on earth.

Jesus wants us to ask for these three things every day. That is why he included them in the Lord's prayer.

Chapter 30 - Fear and Respect God

Jesus said to his disciples:

Do not be afraid of those who kill the body but cannot kill the soul. Rather, be afraid of the One who can destroy both soul and body in hell. Matthew 10.28 Jesus told us to fear God.

But I will show you whom you should fear: Fear him who, after your body has been killed, has authority to throw you into hell. Yes, I tell you, fear him. Luke 12.5

Jesus told us to fear God because He has the authority to banish your soul into hell on judgement day.

He (the angel) said in a loud voice, "Fear God and give him glory, because the hour of his judgment has come. Worship him who made the heavens, the earth, the sea and the springs of water." Revelations 14.7

By fearing God, you show him the respect he deserves. Yes, you can fear and love God at the same time.

Fear God, more than pain, more than death, more than satan, because He has control over all these things.

Chapter 31 - Your Hope and Joy

When you believe in Jesus, God starts a marvellous transformation in your life. Your disposition towards yourself and the world around you, changes. God's Love fills your heart. Every day, you want to seek his Kingdom and his righteousness because when you find it there is an inner joy. You become motivated by God's Love inside you and every day you want to please Him.

All this is for His Glory which He wholly deserves. Your hope is in Him.

If you keep my commands, you will remain in my love, just as I have kept my Father's commands and remain in his love. I have told you this so that my joy may be in you and that your joy may be complete. John 15. 10 -11

Keep Jesus' commands, and your joy will be complete.

Chapter 32 - Absolute Faith

And I (Jesus) will do whatever <u>you ask in my name</u>, so that the Father may be glorified in the Son. You may ask me for anything in my name, and I will do it. John 14. 13-14

You must believe that every word that Jesus spoke was the truth. Jesus will grant you every wish you make, provided that, you have absolute faith that wish will come true and that the wish is for the Father's glory.

Jesus taught us to pray to the Father. To ask the Father. Here Jesus tells us to ask Jesus directly. Therefore, you pray to the Father, but you can also ask Jesus directly to save someone.

My wish is that everybody who reads this will come to a full understanding of the truth that is in Jesus.

Ask Jesus into your heart and Jesus will heal your heart through the Holy Spirit, to the Glory of God, the Father, Yahweh.

Let it be (Amen).

Chapter 33 - God's Generations

We are a generation of people chosen by God.

We are just a generation in the list of generations before the coming of the Lord Jesus.

There were 42 generations between Abraham and the first coming of Jesus. Only the Father knows the number of generations before the second coming. There have been about 32 generations so far. Converting this to time. There was about 5,000 years between Abraham and Jesus. There has been 2020 years since Jesus. How many of thousands of years before Jesus comes again.

We are just one generation of his chosen people. We leave a legacy for the next generation to pass the Word on. We create a foundation for the next generation to build on. in Christ, we are all one.

Your will be done, your Kingdom come in my generation and all the generations to come.

Pray is not limited to the present. you can pray for people who have lived in the past and people who will live in the future. Jesus prayed for you and me.

My prayer is not for them alone. I pray also for those who will believe in me through their message, that all of them may be one, Father, just as you are in me and I am in you. John 17.20-21

Chapter 34 - Discipleship

Throughout the world, there is a network of Christians who have at least two things in common:

They truly believe in Jesus Christ and have received the Holy Spirit. They are one through the Holy Spirit. They might speak different languages live in different countries, but they are one because the Holy Spirit unites them in a common cause. The glorification of God, the Father through the spread of Christianity.

They have the Sword of the Holy Spirit which is the Word of God (Ephesians 6.17).

Jesus said: Holy Father, keep them in your name, the name that you gave me; so that they might be one as we are one. John 17.11

We Christians are one with each other and one with God. We breath as one, we glorify God as one. We are united as one through the Holy Spirit.

Chapter 35 - Jesus' Name

I have come in my Father's name. John 5.43,

Holy Father, keep them in your name, the name that you have given to me, so that they may be one as we are one. John 17.11

God's name is Yahweh. This in Hebrew is יהוה or יהו

Jesus is a derivative of the Hebrew name Joshua.

Joshua or Jesus in Hebrew is יהושע

Notice that יהו (Yahweh) appears in יהושע (Joshua)

It is widely known that Jesus means God Saves. What is not so widely known that the literal translation for the Hebrew name for Jesus is YAHWEH SAVES.

Since the Hebrew word for Jesus contains the Hebrew word for Yahweh. Jesus of the New Testament shares the same name as Yahweh of the Old Testament.

God, the Father and Jesus, the Son have the same name which is Yahweh.

You can check the above meanings of the Hebrew words by copy and pasting them into the Google Hebrew to English translator. You can also go to 'What Does Immanuel mean in Biblical Hebrew?' by Simple Biblical Hebrew on You Tube to find a video which fully explains the logic of the above discussion.

The law was given through Moses, grace and truth came into existence with Jesus Christ. John 1.17

This is the first time that the name of Jesus Christ is used in the New Testament. I believe that John deliberately used the name Jesus Christ so that people understood clearly who Jesus was (the Anointed One).

Chapter 36 – Why does God allow suffering?

I do not know why God allows suffering in the world, but I do know that he has a plan for the world and a specific plan for you.

God has a plan and that plan is for his perfect Kingdom to exist on earth. A Kingdom free of suffering. He wants everyone to find his Kingdom. Satan exists on earth. He is God's enemy, and he wants to control everyone. This is the truth explained in the Bible, which satan does not want you to know.

Jesus answered, the one who sowed the good seed is the Son of Man. The field is the world, and the good seed stands for the people of the Kingdom. The weeds are the people of the evil one, and the enemy who sows them is the devil. The harvest is the end of the age, and the harvesters are angels. Matthew 13.37

So there is a war between satan and God for the souls of the people on earth. God has set the rules and boundaries for the war and satan has limited powers. God lets the war continue because there are still more souls to be saved.

Are you a good person leading a comfortable life without Jesus? Then you are exactly where satan wants you to be and he will not bother you. You are either good seed or weeds. There is no in-between. You have a choice: to receive Jesus into your heart or to continue in sin. Sin is not to recognise Jesus as your Saviour.

Who do you think causes the suffering in the world? Is it God or satan?

Why does God who is full of love, allow satan to cause so much suffering? Why does he protect and heal some but not others? Who are we to question God. Be grateful that he gave you life and use it wisely. The secret of life is to obey Jesus.

Most of the human suffering is caused by man's abuse of power. Wars, starvation and genocide - satan is to blame because he exists and controls most of mankind. Satan is enjoying the power he has over the world right now. He enjoys destroying souls by hiding the truth about Jesus from as many people as possible. If in the process mankind also destroys the planet, he does not care because his days are numbered.

God included in his design of the world storms, hurricanes, earthquakes and tsunamis. They will probably exist in his new Kingdom, but they will not have the power to kill since the souls in the new Kingdom will have everlasting life.

In short, human suffering occurs in the world because satan loves to see it happen. Why God lets it happen? We do not know. But then again, who are we to question God. The question should be, "Why does God allow satan to cause suffering"? God has the power to create and heal, but satan can only destroy what God has created.

There are two types of people in this world. Those chosen by God with the ability to understand God's word, i.e. the children of God. Those that are the sons of the devil who chose not to believe in Jesus. The wheat and the weeds. Which are you?

Chapter 37– Coping with Sadness, Depression, Grief, Guilt and Addiction.

Come to me, all you who are weary and burdened, and I will give you rest. Take my yoke upon you and

learn from me, for I am gentle and humble in heart, and you will find rest for your souls. For my yoke is easy and my burden is light. Matthew 11.28-30

Whatever crisis you are facing now, Jesus is with you. His love surrounds you and protects you.

Next time you are tempted with your addiction or trying to cope with a crisis, say,

Our Father in heaven, in the name of Jesus, please help me. Please send your Holy Spirit to help me through the next minute, the next hour and the whole day. Amen.

Prayer the same prayer for someone you know who is suffering now.

Rely on the strength of the Holy Spirit that is in you to get through this moment.

Chapter 38 – the Tongue

The tongue also is a fire, a world of evil among the parts of the body. It corrupts the whole body, sets the whole course of one's life on fire, and is itself set on fire by hell. James 3.6

But no human being can tame the tongue. It is a restless evil, full of deadly poison. With the tongue we praise our Lord and Father, and with it we curse

human beings, who have been made in God's likeness. James 3.8-9

Your disposition, towards the people around you, is conveyed by what you say. Always be supportive, encouraging and positive in what you say.

Normally, your thoughts come from the heart, overflow into the mind and you speak when you feel in your heart. There are times, when you are stressed or over excited, when you the mind takes control and you speak the first thing that comes to your mind. That is when you might say a lie to get out of an awkward situation or say something negative or hurtful.

For, whoever would love life and see good days must keep their tongue from evil and their lips from deceitful speech. 1 Peter 3.10

Chapter 39- Poor (Destitute) in Spirit

It's the starting point/the launching point from where you start to talk to God. The poor in spirit are ready to talk to God.

It is when your spirit concedes to God recognising Him for who He is. Your spirit is poor because you realise how inadequate and insufficient your life is and how much you need Him.

Lord I need your help today and everyday

Lowly in heart and spirit
Lowly in your innermost self
An inner peace
Meek before God
Trusting him
Yielding yourself to him
Aware of his presence
Safe in his care
Sorrowful for your sins
Sorrowful towards the world
Yet joyful in the Spirit
Open to God
Yet not wanting
Happy in his presence
Content
At peace
Wanting to be righteous
In his eyes
Wanting to please him

Slow breathing
Hypnotic state
Yet wide awake

Touching the Kingdom of Heaven inside you.

Blessed are the poor in spirit
Because theirs is the Kingdom of Heaven

You have just found the Kingdom of Heaven in you.

Chapter 40 - Abraham

And Abraham said, God will provide for himself the lamb for an ascending sacrifice, my son. Genesis 22.8

And then the messenger of Yahweh said, do not put forth your hand unto the young man, neither do to him anything at all, for now know I that one who reveres God you art, when you hast not withheld your son, thine only one from me. Genesis 22.12

Abraham was the first man to find God's Kingdom.

Abraham had complete faith, deep respect and total obedience to God. The three keys to the Kingdom

Those who believe in God, the Father and believe in Jesus Christ his Son and obey their commands, are the descendants of Abraham.

Chapter 41 - Peace with God

Therefore, since we have been justified through faith, we have peace with God through our Lord Jesus Christ. Romans 5.1

On the two occasions, when Jesus met his disciples locked in the room after the crucifixion, he greeted them: "Peace be with you". He never used this greeting before the crucifixion. The crucifixion bought us peace with God. Peace came into existence at the cross. Before the crucifixion, peace did not exist in the world. Isaiah 53.5 says: the punishment that brought us peace was upon him. All those who believe in Jesus have peace with God. It is one of the fruits of the Holy Spirit.

So now that we have Peace with God, what do we do with it? We enjoy it in our quiet moments with Him.

Chapter 42- God's Power in us

God's power in us on earth comes from three things:

The Holy Spirit in us;

The Word of God in us;

The Love of God in us.

How do we unleash this power: BY PRAYER. BY ASKING IN JESUS' NAME

Chapter 43- We are in God

Jesus Prayed: Father, just as you are in me and I am in you. May they also be in us so that the world may believe that you have sent me. John 17.20

This revelation was mind blowing – WE ARE IN GOD. I knew that God was in us through the Holy Spirit, but the thought that I am in GOD is difficult to understand. The only way I can begin to understand this, is to think that my humble spirit is part of the wider spirit world of God.

JESUS IS IN GOD

WE ARE IN JESUS

SO WE ARE IN GOD

AND GOD AND JESUS ARE IN US.

When the Holy spirit enters you, your spirit becomes fused with the Holy Spirit becoming one. You become part of God. Your body is on this earth, but your spirit is now part of God.

Your spirit is a precious gift from God. Look after it while you have it. Although my body is dying, my spirit is alive in Jesus. Jesus Christ has rescued me from this body of death. I am alive in Jesus. My baptism was symbolic of my death with Jesus (the submersion in the water) and becoming alive in Jesus (coming out of the water).

The spirit of a non-believer is not in God and when they die, they lose that spirit forever. A believer receives back his spirit at the resurrection.

My spirit dwells in my body to serve the Lord Jesus Christ, doing the deeds that he has predestined me to do. I must listen to Jesus instructing me through the Holy Spirit which is fused with my spirit to serve God.

Jesus said: I have made you (the Father) known to them and will continue to make you known in order that the love you have for me may be in them and that I myself may be in them. John 17.26

God's Love is in us, and Jesus is in us. The love that God has for Jesus is the same as the love God has for us. That is how great God's love for us is. WOW!

There is therefore now no condemnation to them which are in Christ Jesus, who walk not according to the flesh, but according to the Spirit. For the law of the Spirit of life in

Christ Jesus hath made me free from the law of sin and death. Romans 8.1 and 2

You are FREE to serve Jesus Christ

Chapter 44- God sent Jesus into the World.

Now this is eternal life: that they know you, the only true God, and to know Jesus Christ, whom you have sent. John 17.3

It is important that the world knows and believes that God sent Jesus into the world. It is so important that Jesus mentions it six times in Chapter 17 of John's gospel.

It was God's decision. He could see the mess that we were in, so he decided to forgive us and send. Jesus into the world to save us. To believe in Jesus is to believe that God sent him into the world to save the world.

Chapter 45- Bring Glory to God

Jesus came to earth to teach us to respect and to glorify God, the Father. When Jesus prayed to the Father on the night before he died, Jesus said, I have brought you glory on earth by finishing the work you gave me to do. John 17.4

You can bring glory to God on earth by carrying out the work he has set you to do. That is how you glorify God on earth. Whatever works that God has planned for you, carry them out and you will be glorifying God.

You glorify God in thought, word, and deed.

In thought, when you pray.

In word, when you speak.

In deed, when you act.

For his glory.

You can only glorify God if you remain in Jesus.

Through Jesus, we serve God and bring glory to his Name.

Your whole purpose in life should be to bring GLORY to HIM.

Annex 1 - Evidence there is a Creator.

Fact 1 – The probability of a single cell forming is infinitesimal and if it did form it would have no means of reproducing itself.

The Theory of Evolution says - Life forms came about because chemicals randomly came together in an ancient primordial soup, 3.8 billion years ago to form a single cell by chance.

A single cell is very complex - astronomically complex. A simple one cell bacteria or Coli contains DNA information units that are equivalent to a hundred million pages of Encyclopaedia Britannica. Cells have functional units called proteins. There are thousands of proteins in a single cell. Probability of one protein forming is ten to the power of two hundred and sixty, i.e. impossible.

They still don't know how the first protein was made. The dilemma is that you need DNA to make protein and you need protein to make DNA.

Even if a single cell was formed by chance, how would it reproduce? It would need to develop a method of reproduction in its own lifetime, or the species would die.

Fact 2 - There is no evidence to support the theory that mutations in the DNA chain create new species.

Darwinist Theory - Creatures evolved by mutations causing changes in the DNA chain. Genetics came after Darwin's

Theory, and this is the only way they can explain evolution in terms of genetics.

The DNA of each species is different. Although the DNA of a chimpanzee has 98% of the DNA of a human, that 2% makes a huge difference physically and mentally.

Mutations are rare, but they can alter the DNA structure of a single cell. All known mutations observed so far have reduced the information in the DNA chain. Mutations are irreversibly destructive. There has never been a mutation discovered to date that has added information.

Fact 3 - There is no evidence in the fossil records to support evolution.

All the fossils discovered are of distinct species. No in - between or intermediate fossils have been discovered. We have discovered fish fossils and frog fossils but nothing in-between. There are many breeds of dog, but they are all one species.

Fact 4 - Certain biological systems cannot evolve by successive small changes to pre-existing systems by natural selection.

A single system which is composed of several interactive parts and where the removal of any one part causes the system to cease to function. Examples the immune system, the ear and the eye.

Because the eye system could not occur by evolving from something simpler, it must have been created by a Creator.

This is Irreducible Complexity Theory by Michael Behe.

Fact 5 - Wonderful Earth

Earth is a rare planet and was specially made to sustain plant, animal and human life. When you consider all the factors that came together to create a planet capable of sustaining life, you realise what an amazing creation it is.

Our planet exists in a solar system with a stable sun that has provided a constant source of energy for billions of years. It is exactly the right distance from the sun so that temperatures are not too hot or not too cold. It rotates at a constant speed at the right tilt so that the seasons are not too severe. It has the right amount of retained water to support our environmental weather systems. Jupiter acts like a giant magnet attracting comets and asteroids away from the earth ensuring its survival. Photosynthesis ensures that there is the right amount of oxygen in the air. It has a large moon in the right place to control the tides and oceans. It has the right composition of elements to sustain life especially hydro carbonates. It is as if someone went out of his way to create the perfect environment for plants, animals and of course humans.

Annex 2 – The Nine Daily Dos

Each day I try to do the following:

Glorify Him

Obey Him

Love Him

Fear Him

Respect Him

Serve Him

Trust Him

ASK him

Thank Him

Annex 3 - The Two Big IFS

IF you love me, you will obey my commands. (John 14.23)

IF you obey my commands, you will remain in my Love. (John 15.10)

Annex 4 - The Incredible WE

Jesus replied, "Anyone who loves me will obey my teaching. My Father will love them, and WE will come to them and make OUR home with them. (John 14.23).

Annex 5 - John Chapter 14 Summary

1 "Do not let your hearts be troubled. You believe in God; believe also in me. My Father's house has many rooms; if that were not so, would I have told you that I am going there to prepare a place for you? And if I go and prepare a place for you, I will come back and take you to be with me that you also may be where I am.

6 Jesus answered, "I am the way and the truth and the life. No one comes to the Father except through me. If you really know me, you will know my Father as well. From now on, you do know him and have seen him.

10 Don't you believe that I am in the Father, and that the Father is in me? The words I say to you I do not speak on my own authority. Rather, it is the Father, living in me, who is doing his work.

11 Believe me when I say that I am in the Father and the Father is in me; or at least believe on the evidence of the works themselves.

13 And I will do whatever you ask in my name, so that the Father may be glorified in the Son. You may ask me for anything in my name, and I will do it.

15 "If you love me, keep my commands. And I will ask the Father, and he will give you another advocate to help you and be with you forever, the Spirit of Truth. The world cannot accept him because it neither sees him nor knows him. But you know him, for he lives with you and will be in you.

20 On that day you will realize that I am in my Father, and you are in me, and I am in you.

23 Jesus replied, "Anyone who loves me will obey my teaching. My Father will love them, and we will come to them and make our home with them.

26 But the Advocate, the Holy Spirit, whom the Father will send in my name, will teach you all things and will remind you of everything I have said to you.

27 Peace I leave with you; my peace I give you. I do not give to you as the world gives. Do not let your hearts be troubled and do not be afraid.

Annex 6 John Chapter 15 Summary

1 "I am the true vine, and my Father is the gardener. He cuts off every branch in me that bears no fruit, while every branch that does bear fruit he prunes so that it will be even more fruitful.

3. You are already clean because of the word I have spoken to you.

4 Remain in me, as I also remain in you. No branch can bear fruit by itself; it must remain in the vine. Neither can you bear fruit unless you remain in me.

5 "I am the vine; you are the branches. If you remain in me and I in you, you will bear much fruit; apart from me you can do nothing.

7 If you remain in me and my words remain in you, ask whatever you wish, and it will be done for you. This is to my Father's glory, that you bear much fruit, showing yourselves to be my disciples.

10 If you keep my commands, you will remain in my love, just as I have kept my Father's commands and remain in his love. I have told you this so that my joy may be in you and that your joy may be complete.

12 My command is this: Love each other as I have loved you.

13 Greater love has no one than this: to lay down one's life for one's friends.

14 You are my friends if you do what I command. for everything that I learned from my Father I have made known to you.

16 You did not choose me, but I chose you and appointed you so that you might go and bear fruit—fruit that will last—and so that whatever you ask in my name the Father will give you.

17 This is my command: Love each other.

Annex 7 - John Chapter 17 Summary

1 After Jesus said this, he looked toward heaven and prayed: "Father, the hour has come. Glorify your Son, that your Son may glorify you. For you granted him authority over all people that he might give eternal life to all those you have given him. Now this is eternal life: that they know you, the only true God, and Jesus Christ, whom you have sent. I have brought you glory on earth by finishing the work you gave me to do. And now, Father, glorify me in your presence with the glory I had with you before the world began.

6 "I have revealed you to those whom you gave me out of the world. They were yours; you gave them to me and they have obeyed your word. Now they know that everything you have given me comes from you. For I gave them the words you gave me and they accepted them. They knew with certainty that I came from you, and they believed that you sent me.

9 I pray for them. I am not praying for the world, but for those you have given me, for they are yours. All I have is yours, and all you have is mine. And glory has come to me through them.

11 Holy Father, protect them by the power of your name, the name you gave me, so that they may be one as we are one.

16 They are not of the world, even as I am not of it.

17 Sanctify them by the truth; your word is truth.

20 "My prayer is not for them alone. I pray also for those who will believe in me through their message, that all of them may be one,

21. Father, just as you are in me and I am in you. May they also be in us so that the world may believe that you have sent me.

22. I have given them the glory that you gave me, that they may be one as we are one—

23. I in them and you in me—so that they may be brought to complete unity. Then the world will know that you sent me and have loved them even as you have loved me.

24 "Father, I want those you have given me to be with me where I am, and to see my glory, the glory you have given me because you loved me before the creation of the world.

25 "Righteous Father, though the world does not know you, I know you, and they know that you have sent me.

26 I have made you known to them, and will continue to make you known in order that the love you have for me may be in them and that I myself may be in them."

Annex 8 - 1 John 5 - John's Letter Summary

1 Everyone who believes that Jesus is the Christ is born of God, and everyone who loves the father loves his child as well.

2 This is how we know that we love the children of God: by loving God and carrying out his commands.

3 In fact, this is love for God: to keep his commands. And his commands are not burdensome,

4 Because everyone born of God, has overcome the world. This is the victory that has overcome the world- our faith.

5 Who is he that has overcome the world? He that believes that Jesus is the Son of God.

6 This is the one who came by water and blood—Jesus Christ. He did not come by water only, but by water and blood. And it is the Spirit who testifies because the Spirit is the truth.

7 For there are three that testify:

8 the Spirit, the water and the blood; and the three agree.

9 We accept human testimony, but God's testimony is greater because it is the testimony of God, which he has given about his Son.

10 Whoever believes in the Son of God accepts this testimony. Whoever does not believe God has made him out to be a liar, because they have not believed the testimony God has given about his Son.

11 And this is the testimony: God has given us eternal life, and this life is in his Son.

12 Whoever has the Son has life; whoever does not have the Son of God does not have life.

13 I write these things to you who believe in the name of the Son of God so that you may know that you have eternal life.

14 This is the confidence we have in approaching God: that if we ask anything according to his will, he hears us.

15 And if we know that he hears us—whatever we ask—we know that we have what we asked of him.

16 If you see any brother or sister commit a sin that does not lead to death, you should pray, and God will give them life. I refer to those whose sin does not lead to death. There is a sin that leads to death. I am not saying that you should pray about that.

17 All wrongdoing is sin, and there is sin that does not lead to death.

18 We know that anyone born of God does not continue to sin; the One who was born of God keeps them safe, and the evil one cannot harm them.

19 We know that we are children of God, and that the whole world is under the control of the evil one.

20 We know also that the Son of God has come and has given us understanding, so that we may know him who is true (the Father). And we are in him who is true by being in his Son Jesus Christ. He is the true God and eternal life.

21 Dear children, keep yourselves from idols.

Annex 9   Author's Testimony

The question that I get asked most often while on the internet is, prove to me there is a God. I believe that God only reveals himself to those that he has chosen (predestination), but he has allowed those that he has chosen free will to choose. So, if you are a child of God, you made that choice yourself, although God knew in advance that you would make it. He gives those that he has chosen the ability to feel his presence. You might not realise that you have that ability, or you might not use it, but you have that ability. It took me 72 years to find it and use it. Now whenever I look at a tree or a flower, I can usually feel God's hand in its design and making.

In my young adulthood, I refused to acknowledge his existence and outwardly declared that I did not believe in him. I remember the vicar at our parish church, refused to marry us because I openly declared that I did not believe in God. I remember those that tried to persuade me otherwise. A young Christian girl that I dated, explained her faith to me on Loughor Bridge. A man of God who give me a lift while hitch hiking in Zambia. He philosophy said to me on departing, that one day I would believe. How right he was.

I have always been curious about the meaning to life and in my early thirties, read books relating to evolution of man and the creation of this world. Then in my early thirties I started reading the New Testament. While reading it, without me realising it, the Holy Spirit can alongside me and opened my mind to the understanding of the words I was reading. I wrote what he taught me down in a booklet which I hand typed on one of those manual typewriters. It was only years later when I looked at an old copy of that booklet that I realised that only the Holy Spirit could have taught me those things. I must have at some point asked Jesus or the Holy Spirit to help me and He came into my heart. The Holy Spirit convinced me that I should join a church and be baptised.

Looking back, I wasted the first thirty years of my life and then I wasted the next thirty years. Although a Christian by name and belief, I did not lead a very good Christian life. I was distracted by family, work and my own sexual desires. Satan had me tied in knots without me realising it.

I was frustrated by my life. I wanted to serve him but did not know how. How to serve is something many churches do not teach.   Then at the age of 67 years, I went forward to the front of the church and dedicated my life to Jesus. I gave my heart, spirit, soul, mind and body to Him. I remember because those were the words that I used.

I started talking to God through prayer. I started asking Him questions such as: what is grace? and what is the function of my heart?   Surprising, He gave me answers and I wrote them down in this book.   Words kept coming to my mind day and night and I wrote them down. Many answers came while walking the dog.

He taught me many things, The most important of which were.

.   1.To advance His Kingdom on earth, you need to ASK Him to do things. That is how you serve by ASKING.

2. To remain in Jesus' love, you must OBEY His commands.

3.The WORD OF GOD is so powerful that it not only sanctifies your heart, but also will penetrate the hearts of anyone God has chosen. That is why this book is nearly 25% the Word of God not my words.

 I read about the works of the missionaries in Asia and Africa around the end of the eighteenth century. Many sacrificed their lives and the lives of their families with little success. One missionary in

China took 8 years to find one convert. Many of them spend years translating the Bible into the native language. They would distribute thousands and thousands of leaflets with little success.

In contrast today, you can translate 100 pages in a matter of hours using Google language translator. You can distribute that translation all over the world, within seconds, on social media. Yet very few people are doing this.

Cyberspace is a world of darkness with many false prophets and false teachings. When you find someone teaching the TRUTH, it shines like a light in that darkness. There are also many true Christians on the internet, searching for a way to serve God. I know this because when I send out my Jesus' quotation, I get many likes and encouraging comments. I therefore encourage you, to let your light shine on the internet. Remembering your opinion and beliefs are not important. What is important is the WORD OF GOD that Jesus taught us and asked us to teach others.

PART 2 - To the Glory of God

A Selection of Christian Thoughts and Poems

Foreword

Draw near to God and he will draw near to you. James 4.7

If any of you lacks wisdom,

Let him ASK God,

Who gives to all men generously

And without reproaching,

And it will be given to him. James 1.5

Crucifixion (Is Death by Bleeding)

He had a choice
At any time
To come away
To leave the agony
Of the pain behind.

He chose to stay
To bleed his life away
For that's the price
He had to pay
To buy us back
From him who loves us not,
For Him, who created all we know.

The purpose of the nails
Was to make the blood flow slow,
Down the wood
To form a puddle
On the earth below.

The importance of the blood is that it washes away
All the wrongs
The earth has known.
So now, there
Is no guilt in sin
Only forgiveness
From the one above
To all who know the Son.

Crucifixion Day

That day started at six,
By nine he was nailed and hoisted up.
At twelve the day went dark.
We never expected such a crowd
To see a man, die at three.
It was at that moment,
The sergeant of the guard realised
He really was the Son of God.

By His Wounds We are Healed.

A lot happened at the cross that day.
Yes, he died, so what?

What can one man do
To save a world
That's lost in hopelessness.
Yet he persevered
Knowing the trouble, we were in
And that his sacrifice
Would change the course of time.

Before that day
The fat controller came and went
Owning all he saw
For man had chosen him.

Now there is another choice
For this one man
Has with his blood

Bought us back for God.
By this one act
He heals us of our former sins
Offers a new friendship with God
A new friendship with each other
He can heal our bodies
Our spirits and our fears.
He offers a chance of peace.

A lot happened on the cross that day.

Thoughts

Thank you, God, for inhabiting
The thoughts of my mind.

But let me remember
The seeds you plant within
Are Yours.
And when I think they're mine,
They will disappear
Like the mists of time.

Free Will

For some unknown reason
He has set men apart.
He has made them
In his own image
And given them free-will.
He has even allowed them

The freedom to decide
If he exists.

A Time

A time for sowing,
A time for reaping
A time for waiting and praying
While the seeds grow.

We sow in love
We reap in joy
We pray and wait in hope
Of things to come.

The Truth

Jesus is the Truth
And that Truth
Shall set you free.
Free from everything
That binds you
Physically and mentally.

It starts with a need.
A need to understand
The meaning of everything.
It ends when you find
The Word of God.

Force of Life

There is a force
That is the reason for everything.
It causes plants and animals to grow
It causes the seasons and time.

This force is God
His Spirit is in the grass
 In the trees
In the animals and seas
And is in you and me.

Listen to the force!

For the Asking

He's waiting now,
To see what you're going to say.
What's it going to be?
Can you, will you,
Quietly, humbly, trustingly,
Ask him into your heart,
This man Jesus,
Into your heart to stay.

Printed in Great Britain
by Amazon

44337743R00076